TAKE MY WIFE...

535 Jokes, Riddles, Quips, Quotes, and Wisecracks About Love, Marriage, and the Battle of the Sexes

TAKE MY WIFE...

HUGH PAYNE
Illustrations by Martha Gradisher

**BLACK DOG
& LEVENTHAL
PUBLISHERS**
NEW YORK

ISBN-13: 978-1-57912-597-4

Library of Congress Cataloging-in-Publication Data

Payne, Hugh.
Take my wife—: 535 jokes, riddles, quips, quotes, and wisecracks about love, marriage,
and the battle of the sexes/Hugh Payne.
      p. cm.
ISBN 978-1-57912-597-4
  1. Marriage—Humor. I. Title.

  PN6231.M3P39 2008
  818'.602—dc22

                              2008000139

Cover and interiors designed by Cindy LaBreacht

Manufactured in the USA

Published by
Black Dog & Leventhal Publishers, Inc.
151 West 19th Street
New York, New York 10011

Distributed by
Workman Publishing Company
225 Varick Street
New York, NY 10014

g f e d c b a

CONTENTS

FOR BETTER...
OR FOR WORSE!

Behind every great man is
a woman rolling her eyes.
—Jim Carrey

What counts in making a happy marriage
is not so much how compatible you are,
but how you deal with incompatibility.
—Leo Tolstoy

A m I dating myself by titling this book after Henny Youngman's oft-invoked plea? How many of you reading this even remember the King of the One-Liners, who died in 1998 at the ripe old age of ninety-one? Henny set out to be a violinist and stumbled upon his classic line, "Take my wife . . . please!" quite by accident. He went on to make a pretty good living as a comedian, poking fun at his wife, Sadie, and their marriage, among other things, with brilliant one-liners delivered in rapid-fire succession. Truth is, he loved his wife deeply and she in turn appreciated his hard work. They were happily married for nearly sixty years, and

Henny outlived her by more than a decade. On her deathbed, Sadie implored Henny to continue poking fun at wives and marriage in his act. And, though he felt he'd lost his muse, he did so.

The irony in Henny's story—that he mocked marriage, yet was happily married himself—goes right to the point of this book (if there is one). Marriages evolve as the years go on. The jokes, wisecracks, and smart remarks collected here are organized by the various phases through which every marriage must pass, from the idealistic young love (and lust) of the newlywed to the more earthbound forms of affection that take over as the stork arrives, and then the wrinkles and sags. If you see yourself in any of these jokes, don't be offended. Have a laugh and move on, knowing that you aren't alone.

I can hear a few of you squawking right now, "Hang on there, Hugh. Flossie and I have been married more than thirty years and we're still like newlyweds, sexy and full of love!" To that I say, good for you, Morty. The fact is, while the divorce rate hovers at around 50 percent, gazillions of people are still getting married. There are days when even the most happily married couple can't stand to look at each other, and other days when there's nowhere they'd rather be than sitting side by side on a loveseat, watching *The Apprentice*. That, folks, is marriage.

I dedicate this book to Henny and Sadie, to Flossie and Morty, and to all of you other folks out there (myself included), who are making a go of this rather peculiar institution. Good luck. You'll need it!

Love always,
Hugh

Chapter one
TAKE MY WIFE...
Wedding wit in one line, more or less

Marriage is not a word. It's a sentence, a life sentence.

My wife is an angel.
She's always flying around the house
harping about something.

First guy (proudly): My wife's an angel.
Second guy: You're lucky. Mine's still alive.

Marriage is like a violin.
Even after the sweet music is over,
there are strings attached.

To heck with marrying a girl
who makes biscuits like her mother.
I want to marry one who makes dough
like her father.

A man in love is incomplete
until he has married.
Then he's finished.

It doesn't matter how often
a married man changes jobs;
he still ends up with the same boss.

The three stages of sex in marriage:
tri-weekly, try-weekly, try-weakly.

**My wife and I were happy
for twenty years. Then we met.
—Rodney Dangerfield**

A marriage certificate is just another word
for a work permit.

Why do men want to marry virgins?
They can't stand criticism.

How do you keep your husband
from reading your e-mail?
Name the mail folder "Directions to Mom's."

Marriage is an institution where two people
come together to solve the problems
they never had before they got married.

Marriage is love. Love is blind.
Therefore, marriage is an institution for the blind.

Love is blind, but marriage is a real eye-opener.

"I do" is the longest sentence
in the English language.

What should you give a man
who has everything?
A wife to show him how to work it.

Marriage is an institution
in which the man loses his bachelor's degree
and the woman gets her master's.

Marriage is an institution—
but who wants to live in an institution?

Behind every successful man
stands a surprised mother-in-law.

I married Miss Right.
I just didn't know her first name was Always.

May you be blessed with a wife
so healthy and strong, she can pull the plow
when your horse drops dead.

Marriage is the process of finding out what kind
of person your spouse would really have preferred.

**You know what I did before I got married?
Anything I wanted to. —Henny Youngman**

Why do wives outlive their husbands?
Someone has to stick around and clean up
after them.

What's the difference between
a new husband and a new dog?
After a year, the dog is still excited to see you.

Marriage requires three types of rings:
engagement ring
wedding ring
suffer-ring

All marriages are happy.
It's the living together afterward
that causes the problems.

Marriage is like a bath.
Once you get used to it, it's not so hot.

My wife says I never listen to her.
At least I think that's what she said.

The gods gave man fire and he invented fire engines.
They gave him love and he invented marriage.

**Marriage is like a bank account.
You put it in, you take it out,
you lose interest. —Irwin Corey**

How do you know when your wife is a lousy cook?
She uses the smoke detector as a timer.

Husband: How about a quickie?
Wife: As opposed to what?

Did you ever notice that when you
fall in love you sink into his arms,
but after the wedding
your arms are in his sink?

A recent survey shows that the most
common form of marriage proposal these days
consists of the words, "You're what?!?"

A happy marriage is a matter of give-and-take:
The husband gives and the wife takes.

Getting married is very much like
going to a restaurant with friends.
You order what you want, and
when you see what the other fellow has,
you wish you had ordered that.

Marriage is when a man and woman
become as one; the trouble starts
when they try to decide WHICH one.

What's a husband's idea of helping
his wife with the housework?
Lifting his legs so she can vacuum.

How do most men define marriage?
A very expensive way
to get laundry done free.

**I have learned that only two things
are necessary to keep one's wife happy.
First, let her think she's having her own way.
And second, let her have it.
—Lyndon B. Johnson**

Why do husbands die before their wives?
Because they want to.

How are wives like cars?
On those cold mornings,
you just can't get them to turn over.

What happens when a salesman
marries a saleswoman?
They become sell mates.

Words to live by: Do not argue with a spouse
who is packing your parachute.

Scientists have discovered a food that
diminishes a woman's sex drive by 90 percent.
It's called a wedding cake.

The husband who wants a happy marriage should learn to keep his mouth shut and his checkbook open. —Groucho Marx

Do you know the punishment for bigamy?
Two mothers-in-law.

What happens when a cowboy marries a cowgirl?
It's a Western Union.

Definition of a wife:
An attachment you screw in the bed
to get the housework done.

How are tornadoes and marriage alike?
They both begin with a lot of sucking and blowing,
and in the end you lose your house.

Marriage is a rest period between romances.

**A man may be a fool and not know it—
but not if he is married. —H. L. Mencken**

It's true that all men are born free and equal
—but then some of them get married!

Don't marry for money; you can borrow it cheaper.

Love is one long, sweet dream.
Marriage is the alarm clock.

Marriage is bliss. Ignorance is bliss. Ergo . . .

In marriage, as in war, it is permitted
to take every advantage of the enemy.

Love thy neighbor,
but make sure her husband is away first.

Love: an obsessive delusion
cured by marriage.

**Do not marry a man to reform him.
That is what reform schools are for.
—Mae West**

Shotgun wedding:
a case of wife or death.

Marriage is like a mousetrap.
Those on the outside are trying to get in.
Those on the inside are trying to get out.

Don't marry a tennis player.
Love means nothing to them.

May you be too good for the world
and not good enough for your wife.

May you never leave your marriage alive.

**If variety is the spice of life,
marriage is the big can of leftover SPAM.
—Johnny Carson**

Chapter 2
I Do: Hilariously Hitched
A guy and a gal walk down the aisle . . .

"Congratulations, my boy!" says the uncle. "I'm sure you'll look back and remember today as the happiest day of your life."

"But I'm not getting married until tomorrow," the groom protests.

"I know," replies the uncle.

Courtship, unlike proper punctuation,
is a period *before* a sentence.

Advice for grooms:
Whenever you have a discussion with your wife,
be sure you have the last word: "Yes, dear."

Marriage: a ceremony in which rings are put on the finger of the lady and through the nose of the gentleman.
—Herbert Spencer

**Getting married for sex is like
buying a 747 for the free peanuts.
—Jeff Foxworthy**

Is it all right to bring a date to the wedding?
Not if you are the groom.

How many showers is the bride supposed to have?
At least one within a week of the wedding.

In marriage, the bride gets all kinds of things at her
shower—but for the groom, it's curtains!

What music is recommended
for the wedding ceremony?
Anything except "Tied to the Whipping Post."

A little boy at a wedding looks at his mom and says, "Mommy, why does the bride always wear white?"

His mom replies, "Because this is the happiest day of her life."

The boys thinks about this and then says, "Well then, why does the groom always wear black?"

I was married by a judge. I should have asked for a jury. —Groucho Marx

After six years of dating her steadily, Seymour loves June very much—but he is just too shy to propose to her. The two are both getting along in years and neither has ever been married. One day, determined to propose, he calls her on the phone.

"June?"

"Yes, this is June."

"Will you marry me?"

"Of course I will! Who is this?"

Wedding rings:
the world's smallest handcuffs.

A police officer in a small town stops a motorist who is speeding down Main Street at ninety miles an hour.

"But, officer," the man sputters, "I can explain..."

"Be quiet! I'm going to make an example of you! You're going to cool your heels in jail until the chief gets back."

"But, officer, I just want to say—"

"I said keep quiet! You're going to jail and that's that!"

A few hours later, the officer looks in on his prisoner and says, "Lucky for you that the chief's at his daughter's wedding. He'll be in a good mood when he gets back."

"Don't count on it," says the fellow. "I'm the groom."

A nervous young husband-to-be has some delicate questions for his grandfather. "How often will we have sex, Gramps?"

"When you're first married," his grandpa explains, "you want it all the time, maybe even several times a day. You can't get enough of each other. Later on, sex tapers off and you have it once a week or so. As you get older, you have sex maybe once a month. When you get really old, you are lucky to have it once a year, maybe on your anniversary."

"Well how about you and Grandma now?"

"Oh, we just have oral sex now."

"What's oral sex?"

"Well, she goes into her bedroom and I go into mine. She yells, 'Screw you!' and I holler back, 'Screw you, too.'"

The trouble with some women is that they get all excited about nothing— and then marry him. —Cher

---

Man and wife make one fool. —Fortune cookie

Marriage changes passion.
Suddenly you're in bed with a relative.

Just before the wedding ceremony, the minister notices that the bride is in distress and asks her what is wrong. She replies that she is very nervous, and afraid she won't remember what to do.

The minister says, "There, there. You need only remember three things: first, the aisle, because that is what you'll be walking down. Second, the altar, because that is where you will become a wife. Finally, remember hymn, because that is the special type of song we sing during the service."

The bride nods. As she makes her way toward the front of the church, her family and friends are startled to hear her repeating to herself: "Aisle altar hymn. Aisle altar hymn..."

On their way to a justice of the peace to get married, a couple has a fatal car accident. Soon, the prospective husband and wife are standing at the pearly gates, waiting for Saint Peter to do the paperwork so they can enter. Since they are already dressed for it, they wonder if they could possibly get married in Heaven. When Saint Peter finally comes back, they ask him.

"I don't know," he says. "This is the first time anyone has ever asked. Let me go find out." And he leaves.

The couple is left standing there again. A couple of months pass and they are still waiting for their answer. With all that time to think things over, they begin to wonder whether getting married in Heaven is such a good idea. "What if it doesn't work out?" they fret. "Will we be stuck with each other for all eternity?"

Saint Peter finally returns. "Yes," he informs the couple, "you can get married in Heaven."

"Great," says the couple, "but what if things don't work out? Could we get a divorce in Heaven? Or at least prepare a prenup?"

Saint Peter, red faced, slams down his clipboard. "Sheesh!" he exclaims, "It took me three months to find a priest up here! Do you have any idea how long it's going to take for me to find a lawyer?"

**I always cry at weddings—
especially my own. —Humphrey Bogart**

A girl goes to an ophthalmologist for an eye examination. After he has completed his tests, the doctor says, "Well, it is clear that you need glasses. Be sure to come back after your wedding."

"Why can't I have them now?" she asks.

"Because, miss," he replies sternly, "I don't believe in specs before marriage."

How do you scare a man?
Sneak up behind him and start throwing rice.

A young man excitedly tells his mother he's fallen in love and is planning to get married. "Just for fun, Ma," he says, "I'm going to bring over three women. You try and guess which one I'm going to marry." The mother agrees.

The next day, he brings three beautiful women into the house and sits them down on the couch, where they chat with his mom. After a while, he says, "Okay, Ma, guess which one I'm going to marry."

"The one in the middle," she replies, without hesitation.

"That's amazing, Ma. You're right. How did you know?"

"Because I don't like her."

I'd marry again if I found a man who had 15 million dollars, would sign over half of it to me before the marriage, and would guarantee he'd be dead within a year. —Bette Davis

A young lady comes home looking sad. Her mother asks, "What's the matter, sweetie? Why so glum?"

"Anthony proposed to me an hour ago."

"Then why are you so sad?"

"Well, Mom, he's an atheist, and, um …he doesn't believe there's a Hell!"

"Marry him anyway, dear. Between the two of us, we'll show him how wrong he is!"

All eyes are on the radiant bride as her father escorts her down the aisle. They reach the altar and the waiting groom; the bride kisses her father and both are teary eyed. Before she turns toward the priest, she places something in her father's hand.

The guests in the front pews respond with ripples of laughter. Even the priest smiles broadly.

The bride has given Dad back his credit card.

A wedding is a funeral where a man
smells his own flowers.

A small tourist hotel is all abuzz about an afternoon
wedding taking place there. The groom is a frail
ninety-five and the bride is a vivacious and beautiful
twenty-three. Some are afraid that the wedding night
might kill him.

But lo and behold, the next morning, the bride is
the one looking worn out as she comes down the
main staircase. She is limping and hanging on to the
banister for dear life. She finally makes it to the front
desk, and the clerk says, "What on earth happened
to you, honey? You look like you've been wrestling
an alligator!"

The bride groans, hangs on to the counter and says,
"Ohhh, God! He told me he'd been saving up for
seventy-five years and I thought he meant his money!!"

John and his fiancée, Jill, are a modern couple, quite realistic about the state of marriage these days. They meet with the minister of their church to discuss their wedding vows.

"Pastor," says Jill, "we were wondering if we could make a change in the wording of our ceremony."

"Yes, Jill," replies the pastor, "it is sometimes done. What do you have in mind?"

"Well . . . we'd like to alter the 'until death do us part' section to read, 'Substantial penalty for early withdrawal.'"

Why do architects' brides wear white?
To blend in with everything else in the kitchen.

The only really happy folk are married women and single men.
—H. L. Mencken

A minister is called to a local nursing home to perform a wedding. The elderly but anxious groom meets him at the door. The man of the cloth has a few questions.

"Do you love her?"

"I guess."

"Is she a good Christian woman?"

"I don't know for sure."

"Does she have lots of money?"

"I doubt it."

"Then why are you marrying her?"

"She can drive at night!"

On her wedding night, shortly after consummating her marriage, the bride starts crying.

Trying to console her, the groom says, "What's wrong, sweetie? Are you going to hate yourself in the morning?"

"No! I hate myself now!"

The days just before marriage are like
a snappy introduction to a tedious book.

A man walks into a jewelry store to buy his girlfriend
an engagement ring. Looking at all the offerings in the
glass case, he comes across an exquisite ring with a
large, pear-shaped rock in its center.

"Great choice, sir," the salesman says. "That
particular rings sells for twelve thousand dollars."

"Good God, that's a lot of money!"

"Yes it is, sir. But a diamond is forever."

"Perhaps it is, but my marriage won't last that
long!"

**Bride, *n*. A woman
with a fine prospect of happiness
behind her. —Ambrose Bierce**

Madge: My daughter is marrying a military man: a second lieutenant.
Rose: So, I'm guessing the first one got away?

Why were the ladies who married Orville and Wilbur so happy?
Because they both married Mr. Wright.

He: I proposed to you last night, but I've forgotten whether you said yes or no.

She: Oh, thank God. I knew I turned somebody down last night, but I just couldn't remember who! I wouldn't marry you in a million years!

He: I won the lottery yesterday. I just bought a new Porsche convertible and a beachfront house.

She: My, my! How time flies!

The wedding was in a bathtub.
It was a double ring ceremony.

**Men marry because they are tired,
women because they are curious;
both are disappointed.
—Oscar Wilde**

Did you hear the one about the horny bride?
She carried a bouquet of batteries.

A bowlegged girl married a knockneed boy.
When they stood side by side at the altar,
they spelled OX.

A young man asks his girlfriend's dad for his daughter's hand in marriage.

"So, you want to marry my daughter? Can you support a family?"

"Certainly can, sir."

"Good. There are seven of us."

FAIRY TALE

Once upon a time, a guy asked a girl, "Will you marry me?"

The girl replied, "No." And she lived happily ever after, shopping, drinking martinis with her friends, talking on the phone for as long as she wanted, always having a clean house, never having to cook, filling her closets with shoes and handbags, watching soap operas, staying skinny, and never getting farted on.

The end.

Long engagements give people the opportunity of finding out each other's character before marriage, which is never advisable. —Oscar Wilde

Chapter 3
I DID: NEWLYWEDS
Over the threshold and into the fray

Husband: "Why do you keep rereading
our marriage license?"
Wife: "I'm looking for a loophole."

The newlyweds are suffering from exhaustion and, after an examination, their doctor advises, "It's not unusual for young people to overdo things during the first weeks of marriage. What you both need is rest. For the next month, I want you to limit your sex life to those days of the week with an r in them. That is, Thursday, Friday, and Saturday."

Since the end of the week was approaching, the newlyweds had no immediate difficulty following the doctor's orders. But on the first night of scheduled rest, the young bride finds herself eager as a beaver. Her husband falls asleep, but she tosses and turns, and finally nudges him awake. Disoriented, he asks, "What day is it, honey?"

She looks at him with a gleam in her eye and says, "Mondray."

Love: a temporary insanity, curable by marriage. —Ambrose Bierce

On your wedding night,
when he asks you if he's your first,
think for a moment, peer into his eyes,
and say, "Hmm . . . you might be.
You look very familiar."

The newly married man comes home from work to find his new bride stretched languorously on the sofa, dressed in a negligee. "Guess what I have planned for dinner?" she asks seductively.

"And don't you dare tell me you had it for lunch!"

A newlywed couple arrives at their honeymoon hotel. The manager greets them, offering congratulations: "I want you lovebirds to have a special suite for the night. How about the Bridal?"

To which the wife replies, "No, thanks. I'll just hold onto his ears until I get the hang of it!"

"I have some important news for you, honey," says the newlywed wife to her husband. "Pretty soon, we're going to be three!"

Her husband runs to her and lifts her in his arms, glowing with happiness. He kisses her repeatedly.

When she can finally catch her breath she says, "Oh, sweetie, thank you! I never dreamed you'd be so thrilled about my mother moving in!"

A young couple is out for a drive in the country, but neither of them speaks a word. They've had an argument—and neither wants to give in and apologize.

As they pass a barnyard of mules and pigs, the husband asks, sarcastically, "Are those relatives of yours?"

"Yes," replies his wife. "In-laws."

**Marriage has no guarantees.
If that's what you're looking for, go live
with a car battery.—Erma Bombeck**

A young couple celebrate their first night together, doing what newlyweds do, again and again, all night long.

Morning comes and the groom takes a shower, but finds no towel when he emerges. He asks his bride to please bring him one. When she goes into the bathroom, she sees his body in broad daylight for the first time.

She looks him up and down and her eyes stop about midway. "What's that?" she asks shyly, pointing to a small part of his anatomy.

"Well . . . that's what we had so much fun with last night."

"Is that all we have left?"

On their first night together as man and wife, the newlyweds are getting ready for bed. The bride comes out of the bathroom, all showered and wearing a beautiful robe. The proud husband says, "Sweetie, we're married now, you can open your robe."

She does as he asks—and he is astonished. "Oh, my Lord," he exclaims, "you are so beautiful! Let me take your picture."

"My picture?" she asks, puzzled.

"Yes, my dear, so I can carry your beauty next to my heart forever."

She smiles and he takes her picture, and then he heads into the bathroom to shower.

He comes out wearing his robe and his new wife says, "Honey, why are you wearing a robe? We're married." With that, the man opens his robe and she exclaims, "Oh my! Let me take your picture."

"Why?" he asks, beaming.

"So I can get it enlarged!"

When a man opens the car door for his wife,
either the car is new or the wife is.

The newlyweds are in their honeymoon suite.
As they undress for bed, the husband, a husky man,
tosses his pants to his bride and says, "Here. Put
these on." She slips them on and naturally, they are
way too big.

"I can't wear your pants," she says.

"That's right!" says the husband, "and don't you
forget it. I'm the man and I wear the pants in this
family!"

With that she flips him her panties and says, "Try
these on." He can barely get them up to his
kneecaps.

"Get serious," he says, "I can't get into your
panties!"

"That's right! And that's the way it's going to stay
until you change your attitude!"

An eighty-five-year-old man marries a lovely twenty-five-year-old woman. Because of her new husband's advanced age, the woman decides that on their wedding night they should have separate suites. She is concerned that the old fellow might overexert himself.

That night, she prepares herself for bed and for the knock on the door she is expecting. Sure enough, the knock comes, and there is her gray-haired groom, ready for action. They unite in conjugal union and all goes well, whereupon he takes his leave of her and she prepares to go to sleep.

As she's about to drift off, she is startled by a knock on the door. It's the old guy again, ready for more. Somewhat surprised, she consents to further coupling, which is again successful. The octogenarian bids her a fond good night and leaves. She is close to sleep for the second time when there is another knock at the door. Yes—there he is again, fresh as a twenty-year-old and eager for more. Once again, they do what newlyweds do.

As they're lying in sleepy afterglow, the young bride says, "I am really impressed that a guy your age has enough stamina to go for it three times. I've been with guys less than half your age who were only good for one."

The old groom looks puzzled. "Was I already here?"

A newlywed couple is spending their honeymoon in a remote log cabin resort way up in the mountains. Having registered on Saturday, they have not been seen for five days. The elderly lady running the resort is getting concerned about the welfare of the newlyweds, so she sends her husband to check on them. The old man knocks on the door of the cabin and a weak voice from inside answers, "Yes?"

"Are you okay in there?" he queries.

"Yes, we're fine. We're living on the fruits of love."

"Yeah, I figured as much. But . . . would you mind not throwing the peelings out the window? They're choking my ducks!"

"If you'll just make some toast and pour the juice, sweetheart," says the newlywed bride to her husband, "breakfast will be ready."

"Great, honey! What are we having?"

"Toast and juice."

A newlywed couple returns from their honeymoon, and the new husband decides he'd like to set some ground rules.

"Let's get some things straight," he says. "I'll be home when I want and if I want—and I won't listen to any guff from you. I expect a great dinner to be on the table when I get home from work. Whenever I feel like it, I'll go hunting, fishing, boozing, or card-playing with my friends, and you will never give me a hard time about it. Those are my rules. Any comments?"

His new bride thinks for a minute, then says, "That's fine with me. Just understand that I have one rule of my own. There will be sex here every night at seven o'clock—whether you are here or not."

A knockout young lady decides she wants to get rich quick, so she finds herself a wealthy eighty-eight-year-old man, planning to literally screw him to death on their wedding night. The courtship and wedding go off without any problem, in spite of the six-decade age difference. On their wedding night, she changes into her most bewitching negligee and waits for him to come to bed.

To her surprise, when he emerges from the bathroom he is wearing nothing but a condom to cover a twelve-inch erection, and is carrying earplugs and nose plugs.

"What's all that for?" she asks.

"There are two things I can't stand," replies the old fox. "The sound of a woman screaming and the smell of burning rubber."

Men always want to be a woman's first love. Women like to be a man's last romance.
—Oscar Wilde

Two deaf people get married. During their first week of marriage, they find that they are unable to communicate when they make love. When they turn off the lights, they can't see each other's signing. After several nights of fumbling around and misunderstandings, the wife hits upon a solution. "Honey," she signs, "why don't we agree on some simple signals? For instance, if you want to have sex with me, reach over and squeeze my left breast once. If you don't want to have sex, reach over and squeeze my right breast."

The husband thinks for a minute and signs back to his wife, "Great idea! Now, if you want to have sex with me, reach over and pull on my penis once. If you don't want to have sex, reach over and pull on it fifty times."

Talk about a clueless lover—
this guy waits for the swelling to go down.

After marriage, husband and wife become two sides of a coin. They can't face each other, but still they stay together.
—Hemant Joshi

When the newlyweds get back from their honeymoon, the bride immediately calls her mother.

"Oh, Mama," she says, "the honeymoon was wonderful! So romantic . . ." Suddenly she bursts out crying. "But, Mama, as soon as we got back Sam started using the most horrible language! Things I've never heard before! I mean, all these awful four-letter words! You've got to come and get me and take me home . . . PLEASE, MAMA!"

"Sweetie, sweetie," her mother says, "calm down! Tell me, what could be so awful? WHAT four-letter words?"

Still sobbing, the bride says, "Oh, Mama . . . words like, dust, wash, iron, cook. . ."

I think men who have a pierced ear are better prepared for marriage. They've experienced pain and bought jewelry. —Rita Rudner

Not long after he gets married, Tom meets his father for lunch. "Well," asks Dad, "how is married life treating you?"

"Not very well, I'm afraid. It seems that I married a nun."

"A nun??"

"That's right. None in the morning, none at night . . . none unless I beg!"

The father nods knowingly and pats his son on the back. "Why don't you bring your bride over to the house tonight and we can all have a nice chat?" Tom's face brightens. "Gee, Dad, that's a great idea." "Fine. I'll call and tell Mother Superior to set two extra plates."

After enjoying the events of their wedding night, the newlyweds snuggle in the afterglow. "That was . . . amazing!" the groom gasps.

"I'm glad you liked it. I learned it in the circus," his bride responds.

"Really? I didn't know you were in the circus."

"Yes, I was the sword swallower."

Two neighbors are hanging their laundry on the line. "You know Grace, I notice your clothes never get rained on. It is almost as if you can predict the weather. I think I should start paying attention more, because my clothes are always getting rained on." Grace answers, "You know what, Joyce? Sal helps me forecast the weather. If I wake up and see his penis hanging to the right, I know it's going to be a nice, sunny day. If it's hanging to the left, I know it's going to rain so I hang the laundry inside."

"And what if Sal wakes up aroused?" Joyce asks.

"On those days, I don't do laundry!"

A newlywed husband soon discovers his wife has a problem, so he brings her to the doctor. "My wife is a nymphomaniac," he announces. "She wears me out and then flirts with other men! It makes me very jealous."

The doctor agrees to check her over. He directs her to an examination room and tells her to put on a gown and get up on the table. All the doc has to do is touch her leg and she begins to moan in ecstasy. Caught up in the moment and unable to resist her, he drops his pants and jumps on.

Out in the hallway, the jealous husband hears them going at it. He bursts into the room.

Thinking fast, the doctor says, "Don't get excited. I'm just taking her temperature."

"Doc," the man says, "when you take that thing out, it better have numbers on it!"

A week before his wedding day, the groom, a handyman, falls off a roof and breaks his penis. The doctor carefully sets it and applies a splint to immobilize it. The man doesn't want his bride to worry—so he doesn't tell her about the accident.

On their wedding night, the bride comes out of the bathroom wearing a beautiful negligee. "Be gentle. You know I've never been with a man," she says.

"I have to level with you," he replies. "I've never been with a woman, either. See? Mine is still in its crate!"

The newlyweds are trying to come up with ways to save some money so they can buy their dream house. The husband says, "I've got it. How about every time we have sex, I put a dollar in the piggybank?"

A few weeks later, he decides to count their savings. He opens the bank and pulls out a huge wad of cash. "Where did all this money come from?" he asks.

"Not everyone is as stingy as you are," she responds.

A man breaks into a house and finds a young couple in bed. He orders the husband to get up and ties him to a chair. The burglar then climbs into bed with the woman and starts to caress her and kiss her neck. Suddenly, he gets up and goes into the bathroom.

Seizing the opportunity, the captive husband whispers to his wife, "Honey, this guy's obviously an escaped convict. He's still wearing his prison jumpsuit. He probably hasn't been with a woman for years. I can tell by the way he was kissing your neck. I think you should do whatever he says, satisfy him any way he wants you to, no matter how disgusting that might be. If we make him mad, he might kill us both. Be strong, honey, I love you!"

"Actually, he wasn't kissing my neck," the wife responds. "He whispered in my ear that he was gay, that he thinks you're cute, and do we have any lubricant. I told him it was in the bathroom. Be strong, honey, I love you!"

A pair of newlyweds have been back from their honeymoon only a week when the husband decides it's time he went out on the town with his old buddies. "Honey, I'll be back in a little while," he says.

"Where are you going, snookums?" his bride asks. "I'm going out to the bar, honeybun. I'm going out to have some beers."

"You want beer, darling?" She opens the refrigerator and shows him the assortment of lagers they have on hand. "Which one can I open for you, dearest one?"

"Thanks for the offer, gorgeous, but see, at the bar, they serve it in a frosted glass."

"Oh, you want a frosty glass, my pet?" she asks. She opens the freezer and pulls from it a frosted mug, waiting to be filled.

"That's lovely, dear, but at the bar, it's happy hour and there will be all kinds of hors d'oeuvres."

"You want snacks, Pooh Bear?" She opens the oven door and points to the tray of chicken wings, pizza bagels, stuffed mushrooms, and more that she has been cooking.

"But, sweetie pie," he says, "at the bar, we get together and curse and talk rough and all that." "Sweetheart, why didn't you say so? NOW, LISTEN UP, NUMBNUTS! SIT YOUR LAME ASS BACK DOWN AND SHUT THE HELL UP. DRINK YOUR BEER IN THIS FROZEN FRIKKIN' MUG AND CHOKE DOWN SOME HORS D'OEUVRES. YOUR MARRIED ASS IS MINE AND YOU'RE NOT GOING OUT TO ANY DUMPY GIN MILL. GOT IT, JACKASS?! I love you, hon."

That new contraceptive sponge thingy
is great for married couples . . .
After sex, your wife can get up
and wash the dishes.

**In every marriage more than a week old,
there are grounds for divorce.
The trick is to find, and continue to find,
grounds for marriage.
—Robert Anderson**

Mrs. Harris goes to the grocery store every single day and buys several large cans of dog food. Eventually, the grocer's curiosity gets the better of him. "Mrs. Harris, you must have a dog with a voracious appetite!" he says.

"No, the food is for my husband. I put it on bread and he eats it for lunch."

"My god, woman! You shouldn't do that. You could kill him!"

"Nonsense. He's been eating it for weeks. He likes it and it's easy for me to prepare."

A few weeks later, the grocer sees Mr. Harris's obituary in the newspaper and decides to attend the wake. He approaches the widow and says, "I'm so sorry for your loss. But I warned you that something terrible would happen if you kept feeding him dog food."

"It wasn't the food that did it," Mrs. Harris explains. "He broke his neck trying to chase his tail."

It's their wedding night, and the newlyweds are both virgins. They are in bed, things are getting hot and heavy, and the husband's hairpiece falls off. He reaches around in the bed, hunting for it, hoping his new bride won't notice. His hand accidentally finds its way into her lap.

"Oh, honey, yes, that's it!" his wife moans. "No, that can't be it," he says. "I don't part mine in the middle."

A man goes to the doctor and gets the bad news that he is dying of cancer. He has six months to live, and that's only if he receives heavy doses of chemotherapy.

"Doctor, isn't there anything more you can do?" says the man.

"Well," replies the doctor, "there is one other thing. I suggest you get married as soon as possible."

"Will that cure the cancer?"

"No…but it will certainly make those six months seem longer."

Angela and Mario get married. They spend their wedding night at her mama's house. As this is the first time she has been with a man, Angela keeps running down to the kitchen to ask her mother for advice.

"Mama, he's got hair all over his chest," she says. "That's perfectly normal. Now go back upstairs," Mama assures her.

Angela rushes back down a few minutes later. "He's got hair all over his legs!"

"That's perfectly normal, too. Now go back upstairs to your husband."

By this point, Mario has taken off his socks and Angela sees that he has a club foot. She runs back to the kitchen.

"Mama, he's got half a foot!"

"You stay down here and stir the sauce," Mama says. "I'm going upstairs."

Chapter 4
FIFTH ANNIVERSARY
And baby makes three...four...five

How do we know men invented maps?
Who else would turn an inch into a mile?

The only one of your children who does not
grow up and move away is your husband.

"Dad, is it true? I hear that in China, a man
doesn't know his wife until after he marries her."
"That's true everywhere, son, everywhere!"

Married life is a process.
In the first year of marriage, the man speaks
and the woman listens. In the second year,
the woman speaks and the man listens.
In the fifth year, they BOTH speak
and the NEIGHBORS listen.

A little boy asks his father,
"Daddy, how much does it cost to get married?"
"I don't know, son," the father replies.
"I'm still paying for it."

A man walks into a drug store with his eight-year-old son. They walk past the condom display, and the boy asks, "What are those, Dad?"

"Those are called condoms, son. Men use them to have safe sex."

"Yes, I've heard of that in health class at school," says the child, thoughtfully. He looks over the display and picks up a small package and asks, "Why are there three in this package?"

"Those are for high school boys. One for Friday, one for Saturday, and one for Sunday."

"Cool!" says the boy. He notices a larger pack and asks, "Then who are these for?"

"That's a six-pack for college men," Dad answers. "TWO for Friday, TWO for Saturday, and TWO for Sunday."

"Wow! Then who uses these?" he asks, picking up a twelve-pack.

With a sigh, the father replies, "Those are for married men. One for January, one for February, one for March. . ."

**The most effective way to remember
your wife's birthday is to forget it once.
—Anonymous**

What's the difference between
a pregnant woman and a man?
One has morning sickness,
the other has morning stiffness.

Classified ad: Happy vasectomy, Eric.
Your loving wife and children, Chris, Aida, George,
Carol, Yolanda, Joan, Shirley, Susan, Anita, Aileen,
Jackie, Sheila, Bruce, Dean, Frank, and Maxine.

Husband: Will you love me
when I grow old and overweight?
Wife: Yes, I do.

Four reasons why prison is better than marriage

1. Better food
2. Better sex
3. Occasional shower companions
4. Prisoners occasionally get to finish a sentence.

A father comes home from a long business trip to find his young son riding a brand-new bike. "Where did you get the money for that?" he asks. "It must have cost over three hundred dollars!"

"I earned it hiking," replies the boy.

"Hiking? Come on, son, tell your dad the truth. Whoever heard of getting paid for hiking? Where did you really get the cash from?"

"Dad, every night when you were gone, Mr. Kennedy from the bank would come over to see Mom. He'd give me a twenty-dollar bill and tell me to take a hike!"

When our second child was on the way, my wife and I attended a prenatal class aimed at couples who have already had at least one child.

The instructor raised the issue of breaking the news to the older child. "Some parents," she said, "tell the older child, 'We love you so much we decided to bring another child into this family.' But think about that for a second. Ladies, what if your husband came home one day and said, 'Honey, I love you so much I decided to bring home another wife'?"

One of the women in the class spoke up immediately: "Does she cook?"

A coward is a hero with a wife, kids, and a mortgage. —Marvin Kitman

"You and your husband don't seem to have very much in common," says the new tenant's neighbor. "Why on earth did you get married?"

"I suppose it was the old business of 'opposites attract,'" replies the tenant. "He wasn't pregnant and I was."

FROM A MOTHER'S DICTIONARY

Bottle feeding: An opportunity for Daddy to get up at 2 a.m., too.

Family planning: The art of spacing your children's birthdates far enough apart to avoid financial disaster.

Grandparents: The people who think your children are wonderful even though they're sure you're not raising them right.

Impregnable: A woman whose memory of labor is still vivid.

A man is speaking frantically into the phone, "My wife is pregnant, and her contractions are only two minutes apart!"

"Is this her first child?" the doctor inquires.

"No, you idiot! This is her husband!"

Kate and Tim haven't spoken since the argument they had a few days ago. Instead, they write each other notes.

One evening, Tim gives Kate a note that says, "I have an important business meeting tomorrow. Please wake me up at 6:00 a.m."

The next morning, he wakes up and sees that it is nine o'clock! He can't believe it! Then he notices a note on his pillow that says, "Wake up. It's six o'clock."

**Happiness is having a large, loving, caring, close-knit family—in another city.
—George Burns**

Marriage: the only sport in which
the trapped animal has to buy the license.

Judy and Bill have a big fight and don't speak to each other for days. Finally, Bill breaks the silence and asks her where his favorite tie is.

"Oh, so you're talking to me now?" Judy asks.

"What do you mean?" Bill says.

"Haven't you noticed that we haven't spoken to each other in days?"

"Funny, I just thought we were getting along."

Sign in a marriage counselor's window:
OUT TO LUNCH. THINK IT OVER.

My wife has trouble opening jars.
Apparently, that involves a different set
of muscles than slamming doors.

**Things a husband should not say to his wife
on their fifth anniversary**

➤ Today is our what?

➤ I stopped caring about anniversaries when you stopped caring about cooking.

➤ Okay, let's celebrate. Does it have to be together?

➤ You can celebrate anniversaries with your next husband.

➤ I didn't get you anything. You don't like what I pick out, so I thought, why bother?

➤ If you want me to pretend as if I care about our anniversary, I will.

➤ I thought you only had to celebrate anniversaries while you were still in love.

**I recently read that love is entirely
a matter of chemistry. That must be why
my wife treats me like toxic waste.
—David Bissonette**

Why don't wives blink during foreplay?
There's not enough time.

A man bursts into his house and yells, "Pack your bags, honey, I just won the lottery!"

"Oh, wonderful!" she says. "Should I pack for the beach or for the mountains?"

"I don't care. Just get the hell out!"

Patty is a typical four-year-old girl—cute, inquisitive, bright as a new penny. When she expresses difficulty in grasping the concept of marriage, her father decides to pull out the wedding photo album, thinking visual images might help her understand. As he turns the pages, he points out the bride and groom, the ceremony, the reception, and everything else.

"Now do you understand?" he asks.

"I think so," Patty says. "Is it the day that Mommy came to work for us?"

A woman has the last word in any argument.
Anything a man says after that
is the beginning of a new argument.

A man is in his front yard, attempting to fly a kite with his son.

Every time the kite gets up into the air, it comes crashing down. This goes on for a while, until his wife sticks her head out of the front door and yells, "You need more tail."

"Thanks a lot!" the father yells back. "I told you that last night and you told me to go fly a kite!"

**My husband and I are either
going to buy a dog or have a child.
We can't decide whether to ruin
our carpet or ruin our lives.
—Rita Rudner**

Tanya's husband bought her a mood ring
the other day. When she's in a good mood,
it turns green. When she's in a bad mood,
it leaves a red mark on his forehead.

"Hi, honey. This is Daddy. Is Mommy near the phone?"

"No, Daddy. She's upstairs in the bedroom with Uncle Paul."

After a brief pause, Daddy says, "But, honey, you haven't got an Uncle Paul."

"Oh, yes I do, and he's upstairs with Mommy, right now. They told me to wait down here."

Brief pause. "Uh, okay then, this is what I want you to do. Put the phone down on the table, run upstairs, knock on the bedroom door and shout to Mommy that Daddy's car just pulled into the driveway."

"Okay, Daddy, just a minute."

A few minutes later, the little girl comes back to the phone. "I did it, Daddy."

"And what happened, honey?"

"Well, Mommy got all scared, jumped out of bed with no clothes on, and ran around screaming. Then she tripped over the rug, hit her head on the dresser, and now she isn't moving at all!"

"Oh, my God!!! What about your Uncle Paul?"

"He jumped out of the bed with no clothes on, too. He was all scared, and he jumped out of the back window into the swimming pool. But I guess he didn't know that you took out the water last week. He hit the bottom of the pool and I think he's dead."

Long pause.

"Swimming pool? . . . Is this 265-2854?

The other day, I told my son
about the birds and the bees.
He told me about his mom and the mailman.

"Can I help you?" the woman asks the man browsing through the brochures in her travel agency.

"I have a unique problem," he says. "I vacationed in Hawaii once and my wife got pregnant. While I was on vacation in Spain, my wife got pregnant. And when I was in England, she got pregnant again."

"Maybe you should use protection," the woman suggests.

"Good idea. And maybe next vacation I'll take her with me."

**Having sex is like playing bridge. If you don't have a good partner, you'd better have a good hand.
—Woody Allen**

How many husbands does it take to put a toilet seat down? Unknown. Hasn't happened yet.

What do an anniversary and a toilet
have in common?
Men always miss them.

What would get your man
to put down the toilet seat?
A sex-change operation.

How are husbands like lawn mowers?
They're hard to get started, emit foul odors,
and don't work half the time.

What's the difference between a man
and a lawnmower?
Lawnmowers don't bitch
after they cut the grass.

A man stops a doctor in the maternity wing. "Excuse me, doc. My wife just had a baby. How soon can I have sex with her again?"

"It depends," the doctor says. "Is she in a private room or a ward?"

Soon after a couple turns in for the night, the wife becomes aware that her husband is touching her in an unusual way. Not having had much physical contact with him for a while, she decides just to relax and enjoy herself. He runs his hands along her shoulders, then along her side, across her abdomen, down her leg, then up the inside of her leg. By this time, she is squirming with pleasure. He soon reaches down between her thighs ... then abruptly stops and turns over.

"Honey, why did you stop? I was just getting started."

"I found the remote," he says.

Did you hear about the new
"morning after pill" for men?
It changes their blood type.

Why do black widow spiders
kill their mates after sex?
To stop the snoring before it starts.

**A woman wraps herself in
Saran Wrap to take off some weight.
Her husband comes home, sees her,
and says, "Leftovers, again?"
—Henny Youngman**

Why is sleeping with a man like a soap opera?
Just when it's getting interesting,
they're finished until next time.

What does it mean if your husband is in bed,
gasping for breath and calling your name?
You did not hold the pillow down long enough.

A man isn't thrilled with the way his marriage has been progressing. One day, he storms into the kitchen and announces, "From now on, you need to know that I am the man of the house, the king of this castle, and we're going to play by my rules. Tonight, you're going to cook me my favorite meal and serve me a delicious dessert and coffee. After dinner, we're going to go upstairs and we will have sex any way I want and we won't finish until I say so. Afterward, you will draw me a bath and, while I'm in the bath, you're going to clean up the house. When I get out of the tub, you will be there to towel dry me and rub my skin with moisturizer. Then, guess who's going to dress me and comb my hair?"

"I'm guessing . . . the frikkin' funeral director?"

Why is psychoanalysis quicker for men
than for women?
When it's time to revert to childhood,
he's already there.

**A husband is what's left of the lover
after the nerve has been extracted.
—Helen Rowland**

Why do men have legs?
So their brains don't drag on the ground.

What do husbands and floor tiles have in common?
If you lay them properly the first time,
you can walk all over them for life.

Why did God make husbands?
Because a vibrator can't mow the lawn.

Why do husbands like to masturbate?
It's sex with someone they love.

Why do men wear hair gel and aftershave?
Because they're under increasing pressure from a society that warps their sense of self-worth by reducing them to an assortment of superficial physical attributes.

Or maybe it's because they're ugly and they smell bad.

Man: I know how to please a woman.
Woman: Then *please* leave me alone.

Husband: Shall we try swapping tonight?
Wife: Sure, you stand in the kitchen
while I sit on the couch and fart.

He: Since I first laid eyes on you,
I wanted to make love to you in the worst way.
She: Well, you succeeded.

He: What the hell have you been doing
with all the grocery money I gave you?
She: Turn sideways and look in the mirror.

Man: Your body is like a temple.
Woman: Sorry, there are no services today.

Man: If I could just see you naked, I'd die happy.
Woman: Well, if I saw you naked,
I'd probably die laughing.

Two reasons why men
don't mind their own business:
1. No mind.
2. No business.

Why are husbands like laxatives?
They irritate the crap out of you.

What do you call a good looking,
sensitive, intelligent husband?
A rumor.

A husband is trying to help his wife by doing the laundry. Seconds after setting foot into the laundry room, he yells out to her, "What do I set the washing machine on?"

"What does it say on your shirt?" she asks.

"N.C. State."

A family is at the circus. The young son points at the elephant and asks, "Mom, what's that?"

"That's the elephant's trunk, Billy."

"No, the other end."

"That's the elephant's tail."

"No, THAT," Billy says, pointing demonstratively.

"Billy, that's nothing," his Mom says. Trying to change the subject, she agrees to buy everyone sno-cones and goes over to the refreshment stand. Billy turns to his Dad and says, "Dad, when I asked Mommy what THAT was, why did she say 'nothing'?"

"Apparently I've spoiled your mother," Dad replies.

Why do men whistle while sitting on the toilet?
So they know which end to wipe.

Sammy and his dad are walking down the street. Sammy points and asks, "Daddy, what are those two dogs doing?"

"They're making puppies," Dad answers.

About a week later, Sammy walks into his parents' room and sees Dad on top of Mom. "What are you guys doing?" the boy asks.

Startled at the intrusion, Dad responds, "We're making a baby."

"Could you please roll her over, Dad?" the boy asks. "I'd rather have puppies."

Women need a reason to have sex.
Men just need a place.
—Billy Crystal

**Always be nice to your children
because they are the ones
who will choose your rest home.
—Phyllis Diller**

Little Johnny peeks into his parents' room
late one night—and gets a surprise.
"And you slap me for sucking my *thumb*!"
he hollers.

"You know something, hon?" a man says to his wife, as he steps out of the shower. "It's gonna be a hot one today. I just don't feel like wearing clothes. What do you suppose the neighbors would think if I cut the grass like this?"

"They'd probably think I married you for your money."

The theory used to be,
men mature late, so marry an older man
because they are more mature.
The new theory is that men don't mature at all—
so you might as well marry a younger one.

The gynecologist is surprised to see one of his patients' husbands in his waiting room. "What can I do for you, Mr. Burke?" the doctor asks.

"I'm worried because our new baby has red hair."

"Why is that such a concern?"

"I have black hair, my wife has black hair, and all four of our parents have black hair."

"How often do you have sex?"

"Oh, I guess about twice a year," Burke says, sheepishly.

"That explains it," says the doctor. "The red hair is from rust."

If your wife wants to learn how to drive,
don't stand in her way.

Bachelor: the only man
who has never told his wife a lie.

A Wife's Prayer

Dear Lord,
I pray for wisdom to understand my husband,
Love to forgive him,
And patience to handle his moods.
Lord, I would pray for strength—
But I fear I would use it
To beat him to death.

I must admit, you brought religion into my life.
I never believed in Hell until I met you.

Why do husbands like to talk dirty?
So they can wash their mouth out with beer.

Did you hear about the scientist
whose wife had twins?
He baptized one and kept
the other as a control.

What's the definition of a male chauvinist pig?
A man who hates every bone
in a woman's body, except his own.

Always talk to your wife
while you're making love . . .
if there's a phone handy.

Husband: a man who buys his
football tickets four months in advance
and waits until December 24
to do his Christmas shopping.

**Children should be neither seen
nor heard from—ever again.
—W. C. Fields**

I think of my wife and I think of Lot,
And I think of the lucky break he got.

I tried a mail-order bride,
but she was damaged in the mail.
Luckily, I could return the unused
portion for a full refund.

Why do wives pay more attention to their
appearance than to improving their minds?
Because most husbands are stupid,
but few are blind.

What's a man's idea of a romantic evening?
A candlelit football stadium.

"It's for my mother-in-law," explains the man as he gestures toward the funeral procession, an endless line of male mourners. Tightening the leash, he points down at his dog and says, "My Doberman here killed her."

"Gee . . . that's terrible," commiserates the spectator. "Say . . . is there any way you might lend me your dog for a day or so?"

Pointing again at the queue, the bereaved son-in-law says, "Get in line."

What's the difference between a man and childbirth?
One is an almost unbearable pain
and the other involves having a baby.

Why do so many wives fake orgasms?
Because so many husbands fake foreplay.

I am in total control. But don't tell my wife.

Why did the biblical tribes of Israel
wander the desert for forty years?
Because even back then,
men wouldn't stop to ask directions.

Why do men tend to name their penises?
They feel they should be on a first-name basis with
anything that makes 95 percent of their decisions.

Never have children, only grandchildren.
—Gore Vidal

What's the difference
between a girlfriend and a wife?
About 45 pounds.
What's the difference between
a boyfriend and a husband?
About 45 minutes.

What do you do if your husband walks out on you?
Shut the door.

Never marry a man for money.
You'll have to earn every penny.

Men are all the same.
They just have different faces
so you can tell them apart.

Bachelor: a man who has missed
the opportunity to make some woman
very miserable.

How is Colonel Sanders like the typical male?
All he's concerned with is
legs, breasts, and thighs.

The best way to get a husband
to do something is to suggest
he is too old for it.

Where is the best place in a bookstore
to find a man who is handsome,
faithful, and great in bed?
In the pages of a romance novel.

Why are most men disappointed in the book,
Women Who Love Too Much?
No phone numbers.

What's a man's idea of a perfect date?
A woman who answers the door stark naked,
holding a six pack.

Why would women be better off
if their husbands treated them like cars?
At least then they would get a little attention
every six months (or 50,000 miles,
whichever came first).

Why is it so hard for women to find men
who are sensitive, caring, and good-looking?
Because all those men already have boyfriends.

What is the definition of "making love"?
Something a woman does
while her husband is screwing her.

What do you do with a man
who thinks he's God's gift?
Exchange him.

Why can't little girls fart?
They don't get assholes till they're married.

What makes men chase women
they have no intention of marrying?
The same thing that makes dogs chase cars
they have no intention of driving.

**A man must marry only a very pretty woman in case he should ever want some other man to take her off his hands.
—Sacha Guitry**

How is a man like the weather?
Nothing can be done to change either one of them.

What is it when a woman talks dirty to a man?
$3.99 a minute.

Woman: I want to give myself to you.
Man: Sorry, I don't accept cheap gifts.

Wives dream of world peace, a healthy
environment, and eliminating hunger.
What do husbands dream of?
Being stuck in an elevator
with the Doublemint twins.

A woman marries a doctor. One day he tells her,
"You need to do something to spice up our
lovemaking."

A few days later, he comes home and finds her
in bed with another man who is also an MD.
"How could you do this?" asks her husband.

"You said I needed to spice up our lovemaking;
I just wanted to get a second opinion."

Danny, usually a loving husband, is in trouble. He forgot his anniversary and his wife, Sandy, is furious. "I'll give you one more chance," she says. "Tomorrow morning, I expect to find a gift in the driveway that goes zero to two hundred in five seconds. It better be there, Danny!"

The next morning, Danny gets up early. When his wife gets up a few hours later, she looks out the window. There is a small gift box in the driveway. She put on her robe and goes out to take a closer look. Inside is a brand-new bathroom scale.

An angry wife meets her husband at the door. There is alcohol on his breath and lipstick on his collar. "I assume," she snarls, "that there is a very good reason for you to come waltzing in at six o'clock in the morning?"

"There is," he replies, "Breakfast."

A wealthy man comes home from a gambling trip and tells his wife that he has lost their entire fortune, and that they'll have to drastically alter their lifestyle.

"If you'll just learn to cook," he says, "we can fire the chef."

"Okay," she says. "And if you learn how to make love, we can fire the gardener."

What do men consider foreplay?
Half an hour of begging.

A husband is living proof that a wife can take a joke.

How do husbands sort their laundry?
"Filthy" and "Filthy but Wearable."

How do husbands exercise at the beach?
By sucking in their stomachs
every time a girl in a bikini goes by.

A husband and wife are at a marriage counselor,
trying to resolve their communication issues.
"What's your wife's favorite flower?" the
counselor asks.
"Pillsbury All-Purpose," he says proudly.
The session goes downhill from there.

**According to a new survey, women say
they feel more comfortable undressing
in front of men than they do undressing
in front of other women. Apparently,
women are too judgmental. Men,
of course, are just grateful. —Jay Leno**

A woman hires an artist to paint her portrait.

"When you're all done," she tells him, "add a diamond necklace, sapphire earrings, and a huge emerald cocktail ring."

"Anything you say, madam," the artist replies, "but may I ask why?"

"If I die and my husband remarries, I want his next wife to go crazy looking for the jewels."

The blonde leaves her lover sitting on the sofa when the phone rings, and she is back in a few seconds.

"Who was it?" he asks.

"My husband."

"Uh-oh, I better get out of here!"

"Relax, he won't be here for hours. He's playing poker with you."

Why were men given larger brains than dogs?
So they wouldn't hump women's legs
at cocktail parties.

Ever notice how women's worst problems
can be traced to the male gender?
MENstruation, MENopause, MENtal breakdown,
GUYnecology, HIMorrhoids…

Why are married women
heavier than single women?
Single women come home,
see what's in the fridge,
and go to bed.
Married women come home,
see what's in the bed,
and go to the fridge.

Why does it take a million sperm
to fertilize one egg?
They won't stop to ask directions!

What do you call a husband
who has lost 99 percent of his brain?
A widower.

What is a man's idea of safe sex?
A padded headboard.

My opinions are my wife's, and she says
I'm damn lucky to have them.

My wife doesn't care what I do away from home,
as long as I don't enjoy it.

**I am not the boss of my house.
I don't know when I lost it, I don't know
if I ever had it—but I have seen
the boss's job and I do not want it.
—Bill Cosby**

My wife submits and I obey,
She always lets me have her way.

When you see a well-dressed man,
what's the first thing you think?
His wife is good at picking out clothes.

A husband and wife are lying in bed.
"I'm going to make you the happiest
woman on earth," he declares.
"I'll miss you," she replies.

A couple is in a rut, so they decide to go to a marriage counselor.

"Our sex life is a bore," they say in unison. The husband continues, "We have sex every third Wednesday of the month at eight thirty p.m. I put on Sinatra's 'Night and Day,' we lower the lights, and Kathy lights two jasmine candles and puts on her pink teddy."

"Stop right there," the counselor interrupts. "That's your problem. Everything is too planned, too predictable. You have to be spontaneous, to do it when the spirit moves you. Be more flexible and come back next month."

The couple comes back in a month, and the husband describes what has happened. "Well, we took your advice. We were more spontaneous, went with the flow. We were eating lunch and she gave me 'that look.' We both quickly pulled down our pants and went at it. It was great. Only thing is, we're not allowed to go to McDonald's anymore."

My husband and I are taking Spanish lessons.
You see, we adopted a newborn baby from Mexico,
and when he's old enough to talk,
we want to be able to understand him.

**Never tell. Not if you love your wife . . .
In fact, if your old lady walks in on you,
deny it. Yeah. Just flat out, and she'll
believe it: "I'm tellin' ya. This chick came
downstairs with a sign around her neck,
'Lay on Top of Me or I'll Die.' I didn't know
what I was gonna do . . ." —Lenny Bruce**

Wife: I think it's time we had a baby.
Husband: Let's try getting up every night
at two a.m. to feed the cat.
If that's enjoyable, we'll talk about it.

If women devised the curriculum at men's colleges, the catalog might look something like this:

Bringing Her Flowers Is Not Hazardous to Your Health (or Hers)

Dinner Dishes—Can They Levitate and Fly into the Sink?

Fundamental Differences between the Laundry Hamper and the Floor

Boosting Your Memory Power 101: Birthdays and Anniversaries

How to Fill the Ice Cube Trays: A Step-By-Step Slide Presentation

How to Shop for Hours without Complaint

Is It Genetically Possible to Sit Quietly While She Drives?

Is It Possible to Put the Toilet Seat down Following Urination?

Learning How to Find Things Without Turning
the House Inside Out and Screaming

Loss of Identity: When Your Significant Other
Commandeers the Remote

How to Ask for Directions When Lost

The Stove: What It Is and How It Is Used?

Surviving a Friday Night without Poker or Beer

The Toilet Paper Roll: Can It Replace Itself?

**My wife was afraid of the dark . . .
then she saw me naked and now she's
afraid of the light. —Rodney Dangerfield**

Did you hear about the wife
who said she'd do anything for a mink coat?
Now she can't button it over her belly.

What did the blond wife say
when she found out she was pregnant?
"Are you sure it's mine?"

**If your parents never had children,
chances are you won't either. —Dick Cavett**

Did you hear about the lazy husband?
He married a pregnant woman.

The boss was concerned that his employees weren't
giving him enough respect, so he tried an old-
fashioned method of persuasion: He brought in a
sign that said "I'm the Boss" and taped it to his door.

After lunch, he noticed someone had taped
another note under his: "Your wife called. She wants
her sign back!"

If Men Got Pregnant

➤ Maternity leave would last for two years with full pay.

➤ There'd be a cure for stretch marks.

➤ Natural childbirth would become obsolete.

➤ Morning sickness would rank as the nation's number one health problem.

➤ All methods of birth control would be improved to 100 percent effectiveness.

➤ Children would be kept in the hospital until they were toilet trained.

➤ Men would be eager to talk about commitment.

➤ They wouldn't think twins were quite so cute.

➤ Paternity suits would be a line of clothes.

➤ They'd stay in bed for the entire nine months.

➤ Menus at most restaurants would list ice cream and pickles as an entrée.

➤ Women would rule the world!

**My mother buried three husbands.
Two of them were just napping.
—Rita Rudner**

The husband is not home when he said he would be. In fact, he is hours late, and his wife is alternately angry and worried. Finally, at 3:00 a.m., she hears the front door open, and she walks to the top of the stairs to see him stagger in, drunk as could be.

"Don't you know what time it is?" she asks angrily.

"Don't get excited," he slurs. "I'm late because I bought something for the house."

"Oh really? What did you buy for the house?"

"A round of drinks!"

I never knew what happiness was
until I got married . . .
and then it was too late!

Chapter 5
TWENTIETH ANNIVERSARY
Notta lotta whoopee

How many husbands does it take to change a lightbulb?
One. He sits on the couch, holds the bulb in the air,
and waits for the world to revolve around him.

When a newly married man looks happy,
we know why. But when a man is married twenty
years and looks happy, we wonder why.

Two men are talking and one says to the other,
"You're having an anniversary soon, right?"

"Yup, a big one," replies his friend. "Twenty years."

"Wow! What are you going to get your wife for
your anniversary?"

"We're going on a trip to Australia."

"Australia, that's some gift! That's going to be
hard to beat. What do you suppose you'll dream up
for your twenty-fifth anniversary?"

"Oh, I'll probably go back and get her."

My mother-in-law told me that exercise
helps her burn off calories.
I told her a flamethrower would be quicker.

A man is traveling down a country road when he sees a large group of people gathered outside a house. He stops and asks someone what's going on.

A farmer replies, "Joe's mule kicked his mother-in-law and she died."

"Hmmm," says the man, "she must have had a lot of friends."

"Nope! We all just want to buy Joe's mule."

To be happy with a man, you must
understand him a lot and love him a little.
To be happy with a woman, you must love her
a lot and not try to understand her at all.

Some people claim that marriage interferes with romance. There's no doubt about it. Anytime you have a romance, your wife is bound to interfere.—Groucho Marx

My wife tends to leave well enough alone.
Unfortunately, things are rarely "well enough."

There was once a wife so jealous
that when her husband came home
and she couldn't find hairs on his jacket
she'd yell at him, "Great, so now you're
cheating on me with a bald woman!"

Hubby: You always carry my photo to the office in your handbag. Why?

Wifey: Whenever I face a problem, no matter how difficult, I look at your picture and the problem disappears.

Hubby: Oh, how sweet! I'm so glad I give you strength.

Wifey: Well, it's more like this. I see your picture and I say to myself, "What other problem could be greater than this one?"

I married my wife for her looks—
but not the ones she's been giving me lately!

A husband and wife wake up one morning and the wife says, "I had a funny dream last night. I dreamt that they were auctioning off men's private parts. Big ones were a hundred dollars, medium ones were twenty-five, and small ones went for ten bucks."

"And what about ones like mine?" the husband asks.

"They were giving those away."

"Now that you mention it, I had a dream like that last night, too," says the husband. "They were having an auction of women's private parts. Small ones were a hundred dollars, medium ones were fifty, and big ones were ten."

"And what about ones like mine?" the wife asks, cringing at the answer to come.

"That's where they held the auction!"

He: You know, we've been married twenty years,
but it feels like it's been just five minutes.
She: Oh, how sweet!
He: Five minutes under water, that is.

I just got back from a pleasure trip.
I drove my wife to the airport.

Husband to wife: You know,
I was a fool when I married you.
Wife to husband: Yes, dear,
but I was in love and didn't notice.

**A psychiatrist asks a lot of expensive
questions your wife asks for nothing.
—Joey Adams**

Three guys are sitting at a bar and the talk turns to their wives, and how the women are never interested in sex.

First guy: My wife comes to bed holding an ice cube in each hand and when morning comes, they haven't even melted yet.

Second guy: My wife likes to have a glass of water on her nightstand, but by the time she walks in from the bathroom with it, the glass is frozen.

Third guy: When my wife gets undressed for bed, the furnace kicks on.

At a cocktail party,
one woman says to another,
"Aren't you wearing your wedding ring
on the wrong finger?"
Replies her friend, "Yes, I am.
I married the wrong man."

A woman tells her friend,
"It is I who made my husband a millionaire."
"And what was he before you
married him?" the friend inquires.
"A billionaire."

You know, if it weren't for marriage,
men would go through life thinking
they had no faults at all.

What's the worst thing a woman can get
on her twentieth wedding anniversary?
Morning sickness.

**I've had bad luck with both wives.
The first one left me and the second one
didn't. —Patrick Murray**

A woman married for twenty years dies and her husband plans an elaborate funeral. At the end of the service, the pallbearers are carrying the woman's remains out to the waiting hearse when they accidentally bump into a wall, jarring the casket.

They hear a faint moan. They quickly open the coffin and—miracle of miracles—the woman is actually alive!

She lives another ten years and then dies. Her husband again plans a beautiful funeral ceremony. When it is over and the pallbearers are again carrying out the casket, the husband yells, "Look out for the wall!"

A husband and wife are shopping when the wife says, "Darling, it's my mother's birthday tomorrow. What shall we buy for her? She would like something electric."

Replies the husband, "How about a chair?"

Bigamy is having one wife too many.
Monogamy is the same.—Oscar Wilde

"The thrill is gone from my marriage," Bill tells his friend Doug.

"Why not add some intrigue to your life and have an affair?" Doug suggests.

"But what if my wife finds out?"

"Heck, this is a new age we live in, Bill. Go ahead and tell her about it!"

So Bill goes home and says, "Dear, I think an affair will bring us closer together."

"Forget it," says his wife. "I've tried that—it's never worked."

Why did God make Adam before Eve?
You need to make a rough draft
before you make the final version.

Mike needs to call home, but his cell phone is dead and a man is using the only pay phone around. So he stands and waits his turn, assuming it will only be a couple of minutes.

Five minutes pass, and the man is still on the phone—or at least he is holding the phone. He never utters a word.

Ten minutes later, same scenario.

After a few more minutes, Mike gets impatient. Is the guy in a coma or in shock or something? He taps him on the shoulder and says, "Excuse me a second. Can I use the phone real quick? I won't be long. I just need to make an important call."

With that, the guy covers the receiver with his hand and says, "Relax, bud, hold your horses. I'm talking to my wife."

I had some words with my wife.
Then she had some paragraphs with me.

How many men does it take to open a beer?
None. It should be open when your wife
brings it to you.

How many wives does it take
to change a lightbulb?
None. They'd rather sit in the dark and bitch.

How can you tell if your wife is dead?
The sex is the same but the dishes pile up.

In the beginning, God created the earth and rested.
Then God created Man and rested.
Then God created Woman.
Since then, neither God nor Man has rested.

Why does it take wives longer to climax?
Who cares?

Why are your wife's feet smaller than yours?
It's evolution. Smaller feet
allow her to stand closer to the sink.

When do you know a woman
is about to say something smart?
When she starts a sentence with,
"My husband once said . . ."

How can you tell if your husband is dead?
The sex is the same,
but you get to use the remote.

How do you set your wife's watch?
Doesn't matter. There's a clock on the oven.

Why do husbands pass more gas than wives?
Because wives can't shut up long enough
to build up the required pressure.

If your dog is barking at the back door
and your wife is yelling on the front porch,
who should you let in first?
Your dog. He'll shut up once you let him in.

Women will never be equal to men
until they can walk down the street
with a bald head and a beer gut,
and still think they are sexy.

Adam was wandering aimlessly through the Garden of Eden looking depressed, so God asked him what was wrong.

Adam complained that he was lonely, he had no one to talk to.

So, God decided that he would give him a companion called "woman." "This person will cook for you and wash your clothes," God explained. "She will always agree with every decision you make. She will bear your children. She will not nag you, and she will be the first to admit she is wrong during every argument. Finally, she will freely give you love and pleasure whenever you need them."

Adam says, "That sounds great, God. What will this woman cost me?"

"An arm and a leg," God answers.

"Hmmm. What can I get for just a rib?"

And the rest is history.

Adam and Eve had an ideal marriage.
He didn't have to hear about all the men
she could have married, and she didn't have
to hear about the way his mother cooked.

How can you tell good mushrooms
from bad ones?
Serve them to your mother-in-law.
If she drops dead, they're good.

**The most happy marriage I can
imagine to myself would be the union
of a deaf man to a blind woman.
—Samuel Taylor Coleridge**

Personally, I know nothing about sex because I have always been married.
—Zsa Zsa Gabor

A wife is making breakfast for her husband when he bursts into the kitchen. "Careful!" he shouts. "There's too much grease in that bacon pan! Is that bacon burning?! Watch those eggs. Don't you think they should be turned over?! Oh my God, it looks like they're burning! What's that I smell?! Is the toast on fire?! I don't think there's enough butter in that pan! Oh no, where is the pot holder?!"

The wife turns and looks him in the eye. "What the heck is wrong with you? Don't you think I know how to make breakfast?"

"I just want you to see what it feels like when I'm driving."

My wife wants to try the missionary position. She'll be on top—and I'll be in Africa.

Sign on delivery truck:
This driver carries no money.
His wife has it all.

Wife: The perfect acquisition for any gentleman feeling himself to have excessive control over his personal affairs.

A guy gets a telegram informing him of his mother-in-law's death, and inquiring as to whether she should be buried or cremated.

"Don't take any chances," he replies. "Burn the body and bury the ashes."

Sam is invited to his friend Dave's house for dinner. He notices that every time Dave needs something from his wife, he precedes his request with "my love," "darling," "sweetheart," etc.

Sam says to Dave, "Wow, that's really nice. After twenty years of marriage, you still use little pet names and endearments."

"Well, honestly," says Dave, "I've forgotten her name."

"Honey," says a husband to his wife, "I invited a friend home for supper."

"What? Are you crazy? The house is a mess, I haven't been shopping, all the dishes are dirty, and I don't feel like cooking a fancy meal!"

"I know all that."

"Then why did you invite a friend for supper?"

"Because the poor fool's thinking about getting married."

A man is riding his motorcycle along Malibu Beach one morning when he spots something glimmering in the sunlight—it's the proverbial magic lamp! He's read all the old stories, so he promptly rubs the lamp and—sure enough—in a puff of smoke, out pops a genie!

"You have released me from my tomb. For that, I will grant you one wish," the genie declares.

The biker thinks about it, then says, "Build me a bridge to Hawaii so I can ride there anytime I want."

"That would be impossible," replies the genie. Do you know how far away Hawaii is from here? It would be a logistical nightmare to get together that much asphalt and manpower. And think of the environmental impact. Why don't you take a little more time and think of a better wish, maybe one that would benefit mankind as a whole."

The man thinks for awhile, then says, "Like all men, I'd really like to understand my wife better. I'd like to know how to make her truly happy. Can I wish for that?"

"How many lanes do you want on that bridge?"

**Woman inspires us to great things,
then prevents us from achieving them.
—Alexandre Dumas**

If you want your spouse to listen and pay attention
to every word you say, talk in your sleep.

When a man holds a woman's hand
before marriage, it's love;
after marriage it's self-defense.

A woman posts a personal ad that reads,
"Husband wanted." The next day she
receives hundreds of letters, all saying
the same thing: "You can have mine!"

Losing a wife can be hard.
In my case, it was almost impossible.

It's Jim's last day as a mail carrier, after thirty-five years. All of the people on his route are aware of it and want to express their appreciation for his many years of service. At one house, everyone in the family greets him at the door, hugs him, and gives him a nice gift envelope. All along the route, people shower him with cash, cigars, food, even football tickets.

At the last house on his route, he is met at the door by a gorgeous blond wearing a revealing negligee. She takes Jim by the hand, leads him upstairs, and makes passionate love to him. Afterward, she brings him down to her kitchen and fixes him a gourmet lunch. Jim hungrily devours the meal and, as he reaches for the glass of vintage wine she has set in front of him, he notices a dollar sticking out from under the glass. He says to his hostess, "This has been . . . an absolutely wonderful afternoon—but I'm curious. What's the dollar for?"

"Last night," replies the blond, "I told my husband that today would be your last day as our mailman. I suggested that we do something special for you. I asked him if he had any ideas. He said, 'Screw him. Give him a dollar.' The lunch was my idea!"

You know that "look" women get when they want sex? Me neither.
—Steve Martin

Many a wife thinks her husband is the world's greatest lover, but few ever catch him at it.

When you want a man to play with you, wear a full-length black nightgown with buttons all over it. Sure, it's uncomfortable, but it makes you look just like his remote control.

One day, a man comes home and is greeted
by his wife dressed in a sexy nightie.
"Tie me up," she purrs, "and do anything you want."
So he ties her up and goes golfing.

A guy is sitting at a bar when a second guy comes in, puts a paper bag on the bar, and orders himself a beer.

"What's in the bag?" the first guy asks.

"It's a six-pack of wine coolers. I got them for my wife."

"Good trade," guy number one nods.

Two married fellas, Jim and Alec, are having a beer after work. Jim says, "Have you ever said something when you meant to say something else?"

"How do you mean?" asks Alec.

"Okay, for example, the other day, I was at the travel agent's and instead of asking for two tickets to Pittsburgh, I said 'Give me two pickets to Titsberg.'"

"Oh, yeah, I know what you mean," says Alec. "Last week I was having breakfast with my wife. I meant to say, 'Honey, please pass me the sugar,' but what came out was, 'You ruined my life, you BITCH!'"

What do you call a wife who can suck
a golf ball through fifty feet of garden hose?
Darling.

A man walks into his bedroom and sees his wife
packing a suitcase. "What are you doing?" he asks.

"I'm moving to Las Vegas. I heard that ladies-of-
the-night there get paid four hundred dollars for
doing what I do for you for free."

Later that same evening, the wife walks into the
bedroom and sees her husband packing his suitcase.
"Where do you think you're going?" she asks.

"I'm going to Vegas, too. I want to see you live on
eight hundred dollars a year."

Every time I find Mr. Right,
my husband scares him away.

Before marriage,
a man declares that he would
lay down his life to serve you.
After marriage,
he won't even lay down his
newspaper to talk to you.
—Helen Rowland

A woman is a complicated creature.
Before marriage, she expects a man,
after marriage she suspects him,
and after death she respects him.

Here lies my wife in earthy mould.
When she lived she did naught but scold.
Good friends go softly in your walking
Lest she should wake and rise up talking.

Why is a laundromat a really
bad place to find a wife?
Because a woman who can't
even afford a washing machine
will never be able to support you.

A woman is paying for some purchases at Macy's. As she reaches for her debit card, a television remote control falls out of her purse. The checkout girl asks, "Do you always carry your TV remote?"

"No," the woman responds, "but my husband refused to come shopping with me today. I figured this was a great way to pay him back."

Never do housework.
No man ever made love to a woman
because the house was spotless.

Joint checking account: a handy little device that permits your wife to beat you to the draw.

A drunk walks into a bar, crying. He sits down on the closest stool and says to the bartender, "I did a horrible thing earlier tonight. I traded my wife for a bottle of Scotch."

"That's awful," says the barkeep. "I bet you're sorry, and now you want to get her back because you love her and miss her—right?"

"Actually, no. I want her back because I'm thirsty again."

Honolulu: It's got everything.
Sand for the children, sun for the wife,
sharks for the wife's mother . . .
—Ken Dodd

A guy leaves for work but, when he is about a mile from home, he realizes that he's left some important papers on his desk in the bedroom. He drives back home, and as he walks into the bedroom, he sees his wife lying naked in a compromising position and the milkman, also naked, standing at the side of the bed. When he spies the husband, the milkman quickly squats over the rug.

"I'm so glad you're here, Mr. Baker," he says. "I was just telling your wife that if she didn't pay the bill for her milk bath, I would crap on your rug."

A guy comes home earlier than planned from a business trip and finds his wife in bed with the mailman. Furious, he yells, "Suzi, what the hell are you doing?!"

Suzi turns to her lover and says, "See? I told you he was stupid."

Suspecting infidelity, a guy barges in on his wife
in the middle of the day. Sure enough, she is in bed
with a naked man. "I knew it!" he shouts. "I'm gonna
kill that bastard!" He starts rifling through his nightstand, looking for his revolver.

"Don't shoot, Max!" his wife yells. "Who do you
think paid for our Jaguar and our shore house?!"

"Oh my God," Max replies. "Don't let him catch
cold. Can we get you anything to make you more
comfortable, buddy?"

Dumb Dan suspects his wife, Hot Helen, is cheating on
him. He purposely comes home early one day, bursts
into the bedroom, and, wouldn't you know it?
There's Hot Helen in bed with Johnny, the UPS man.
In a suicidal frenzy, Dan reaches into his nightstand,
pulls out his revolver, and points it at his own head.

"Don't laugh," he yells at Helen. "You're next!"

My wife worries so much about her clothes
being stolen. I came home yesterday after lunch
and I met the guy she's hired to guard her stuff.
He was standing naked in her closet.

A husband and wife are having sex when the man
stops what he's doing and asks, "Are you okay? Are
you not feeling well?"

"I'm fine," she says breathlessly. "Why do you ask?"

"I thought you moved."

The definition of mixed emotions?
Your mother-in-law driving over a cliff
in your new Porsche.

Husband: Why do you iron your bra
when you have nothing to put into it?
Wife: I iron your boxers, don't I?

**Someone stole all my credit cards,
but I won't be reporting it.
The thief spends less than my wife did.
—Henny Youngman**

Milt goes to the doctor and explains that, after twenty years of marriage, his sex life isn't all it could be. He is hoping the doctor might be able to prescribe a pill that will get him aroused. The doctor has just the right medication, so Milt takes a pill and drives home.

When he walks in the door, he discovers that his wife is out. He waits for over an hour with a tent in his pants, and finally alleviates his "pain" himself.

The doctor calls the next day to check on him, and Milt explains what had happened. "You know, Milt," the doctor says, "you didn't have to do it yourself, there are other women in town."

"Doc, for other women I don't need a pill," Milt says.

A husband has a problem with premature ejaculation. The local sex shop gives him a can of stay-hard spray. The label on the can promises that if you spray a little of it on, you can go all night.

The man goes home and hides the can in a cabinet. After dinner, anticipating a night of passion with his wife, he applies the spray. They begin making love—but he finishes faster than ever. The next day, he takes the can back to the sex shop for a refund.

"Let me guess," the sales clerk says. "You brought the can home and hid it in the kitchen cabinet?"

"Right! How did you guess?"

"You must have grabbed the can of EZ Off, instead."

My wife is an earth sign.
I'm a water sign.
Together, we make mud.
—Henny Youngman

The husband grabs his wife's buttocks as she steps out of the shower and says, "You know, if you firmed these up a little, you wouldn't have to wear a girdle." His wife's feelings are hurt, but she doesn't say anything.

About a week later, she is again stepping out of the shower and her husband walks in. He grabs her breasts and says, "You know, if you firmed these up, you wouldn't have to wear an underwire bra."

At this point, she's had enough. The next time he takes a shower, she is waiting for him as he steps out to dry off. She grabs him between his legs and says, "You know honey, if you firmed this up a bit, I wouldn't have to keep using the FedEx guy."

Vivian and Myrtle are sitting on the porch and Viv says, "Joe came home with a dozen roses today. I guess I'll have to spend the weekend with my legs in the air."

"Vivian!" replies Myrtle. "Don't you own a vase?"

Phil comes home drunk one night and slips quietly into bed next to his wife. He falls into a deep sleep and has a strange dream. He dreams that he has died and, after heavy protest, St. Peter gives him a second chance to live. "But, there's one condition," says the heavenly gatekeeper. "You have to go back as a chicken."

Phil isn't happy about this, but he figures, well, life is life—and maybe living on a nice farm won't be too bad. He soon find himself covered with feathers and pecking around a farm.

Soon, he experiences a strange feeling he doesn't understand. He asks the other chickens about it.

"It's no big deal," one of the other hens tells him. "You're just ovulating. Happens to me all the time. Sheesh, you act like you've never laid an egg or something. Just relax and let nature take its course." Phil takes a few deep breaths, tries to relax, and a minute or so later, out pops an egg. That one is followed by another, and soon Phil understands the joy a woman feels when she gives birth. He tries to push out a third egg, when, suddenly, he feels a smack on the head.

"Phil, you idiot! Wake up! You've crapped the bed!"

A wife observes the couple next door: "Do you see the Schwartzes? How devoted they are to each other? He kisses her every time they meet. Why don't you do that?"

"I would love to," replies the husband, "but I don't think I know her well enough."

A husband and wife are lying in bed one night, reading. "It says here," the wife points out, "that women use approximately thirty thousand words a day, while men use about fifteen thousand. That's probably because women have to repeat everything to men."

Her husband turns to her and says, "Wha'?"

Did you hear about the new Husband Store that just opened in Times Square? It is designed so that women can go there to choose a husband. Here's how it works: You can visit the store only once. There are six floors, and the quality of the selections increases as you move up from floor to floor. You can choose a man at any point, or you can choose to go up to the next floor, but you can't go down unless you go all the way down to the exit.

Kim knows the rules when she visits the Husband Store. She starts on the ground floor, where a sign says, "These men have jobs." She decides to continue upward.

Second floor: "These men have jobs and love kids." Mmm, not yet, Kim decides.

Third floor: "These men have jobs and love kids and are extremely handsome." Feeling at once greedy and excited, Kim keeps climbing.

Fourth floor: "These men have jobs and love kids and are extremely handsome and help with homework." She almost stops there—but she just can't help herself. She decides to go further.

Fifth floor: "These men have jobs and love kids and are extremely handsome and help with homework and are great lovers." Wow. Tempting. But yet again, Kim takes her chances. There's still one more floor.

On Six, she is greeted by a digital automated sign that reads, "You are visitor number 8,756,013 to the sixth floor. There are no men here. This floor exists solely as proof that women are impossible to please. Thank you for shopping at the Husband Store."

A couple is arguing about who should make the coffee in the morning. The wife says, "I think you should do it because you get up first."

He counters with, "The kitchen is your domain— you do all the cooking so you know where everything is. I think you should make the coffee."

"No way," she says. "You should do it. The Bible even says so."

"What the heck are you talking about?"

She grabs the family Bible, thumbs through, and points to the appropriate section: "Hebrews."

**When a man steals your wife,
there is no better revenge than to
let him keep her. —Sacha Guitry**

A couple goes out for their twentieth anniversary dinner. After their meal, they return home to discover that their kids have prepared a surprise for them. The table is set, the candles are lit, and there is a note on the table:

"Your dessert is in the refrigerator. We're staying at friends' houses, so go ahead and do something that we wouldn't do!"

The wife turns to her husband and says, "I guess we could vacuum."

He: How can you be so pretty but be so stupid?
She: It's simple. God made me beautiful
so you'd be attracted to me. God made
me stupid so I'd be attracted to you!

A long-in-the-tooth couple decides they'll try to rekindle a sense of romance by taking a camping trip together. They brush up on the topic by reading books on camping and outdoor survival. They buy some new equipment and venture out to the closest National Park.

The trip is going fairly well until the third day, when they are hiking over a ridge and come upon a five-hundred-pound grizzly bear. The bear starts toward them and the man begins to run.

"Why are you running?" his wife asks. "It says in the book that you should stand completely still and make loud noises if you see a bear! It does no good to run because you can never outrun a bear!"

"I don't have to outrun the bear," he yells back to her. "I just have to outrun you!"

All men make mistakes, but married men find out about them sooner. —Red Skelton

The gynecologist examining Mrs. Weber looks up. "I'm sorry, but removing that vibrator will involve a very lengthy and delicate procedure. We'll have to admit you to the hospital."

"I'm not sure my husband's insurance will cover it," Mrs. Weber says. "Why don't you just replace the batteries?"

My wife and I got into a conversation about life and death and the purpose of living wills. I told her I never want to exist in a vegetative state, having to depend on some machine and getting nourishment from a bottle.

She got up, unplugged the TV, and dumped my beer down the sink.

Marriage is a matter of give and take, but so far I haven't been able to find anybody who'll take what I have to give. —Cass Daley

You know the honeymoon is pretty much over
when you start to go out with the boys
on Wednesday nights—and so does she.

Sal complains of a headache. Mario says, "Do what I do. I put my head on my wife's bosom and the headache goes away."

The next day, they cross paths again and Mario asks, "Did you do what I told you to?"

"Yes, I sure did. Worked like a charm. By the way, you have a nice house!"

EXCERPTS FROM THE
WOMAN'S DICTIONARY
(as compiled by a man)

At your convenience:
This usually precedes a request from your wife about a chore she would like you to do. It really means NOW.

Fine:
The word women use to end an argument when they still think they are right but want you to shut up.

Five minutes:
Means half an hour when used as a response to the question, "How long before you are ready to go?" It is equivalent to the TWO minutes that your football game is going to last before you do what she's asked, so it's an even trade.

Go ahead (with raised eyebrows):
This is a dare. Don't do it!

Go ahead (normal eyebrows):
This means "I give up" or "do what you want because I don't care anymore."

I got it, don't worry about it:
You're in trouble. She asked you to do "it" and you didn't, so now she has to handle it. And God help you if she screws "it" up or gets hurt in the process.

Loud sigh:
This is not actually a word, but a nonverbal statement often misunderstood by men. It means she thinks you are an idiot and wonders why she is even wasting her time standing here arguing with you.

Soft sigh:
Another nonverbal statement meaning that she is content. If you don't move, breathe, or say anything, maybe she'll stay content. Maybe not.

Nothing:
This means "something." Be on your toes.

Thanks:
No hidden meaning—a woman is thanking you. Just say "you're welcome."

Thanks a lot:
This is much different from "Thanks." You have offended her and she is really ticked off at you.

That's Okay:
She wants to think long and hard before paying
you back for whatever it is that you have done.
At some point in the near future, you are probably
going to be in some mighty big trouble.

Whatever:
A rough translation would be "@#$^&@ you."

WHY IT'S GOOD TO BE A MAN

Wedding plans take care of themselves.

Your last name stays the same.

Wedding dress: $3,000; tux rental: $80.

The garage is your domain and yours alone.

You know stuff about tanks and motorcycles.

You can wear a white shirt to a water park.

You could care less if someone
notices your new haircut.

Wrinkles and gray hair add character.

Christmas shopping on December 24
for twenty relatives in under ninety minutes.

People rarely glance at your chest
when you talk to them.

Car mechanics tell you the truth.

The occasional belch and/or fart
is expected.

One mood, all the time.

Phone conversations can be completed
in less than thirty seconds.

A five-day vacation requires just one suitcase
and ten minutes to pack.

The world is your urinal.

You can open your own jars.

WHAT MEN SAY
AND WHAT THEY REALLY MEAN

Can I help with dinner?
Why isn't it on the table already?

I *do* help around the house!
I once picked up my dirty socks.

I don't need instructions.
I'm fully capable of screwing this up myself.

I'm getting more exercise lately.
The batteries in the TV remote are dead.

It would take too long to explain.
I have no idea myself but I won't admit it.

We're going to be late!
Now I have a legitimate excuse to drive like a maniac.

Take a break, sweetie, you're working too hard.
I can't hear the game over the drone of the vacuum.

That's interesting dear.
Are you still talking?

Chapter 6
FIFTIETH ANNIVERSARY
Please pass the Viagra

Old wife: Let's go upstairs and make love.
Old husband: Honey, I can't do both!

Two deaf old men are in a coffee shop discussing their wives.

One signs to the other: "Boy, was my wife mad at me last night! She kept going on and on and wouldn't stop!"

"When my wife goes off on me, I just don't listen," his buddy signs.

"How do you get away with that?"

"It's easy! I turn off the lights!"

Old Farmer Johnson is dying and his family is standing around his bed. In a barely audible voice, he says to his wife, "When I'm dead, I want you to marry Farmer Jones."

"Oh, honey, I can't marry anyone after you," the grief-stricken wife responds.

"But I want you to," he assures her.

"But why?"

"Jones once cheated me in a horse deal!"

People are always asking me the secret of my long and happy marriage. Here's the truth. My wife and I make a point of going out twice a week to a nice restaurant. We enjoy some good food, a little candlelight, some soft music, and a pleasant walk home.

The missus goes Tuesdays; I go Fridays.

As he lay on his deathbed, a man confides to his wife, "I cannot die without telling you the truth. I cheated on you throughout our entire marriage. All those nights when I told you I was working late? I was with other women. Not just a few women either; I've slept with dozens of them."

His wife looks at him calmly and says, "Why do you think I gave you the poison?"

A man is lying on his deathbed. His wife asks him, "Is there anything I can get you, Mortie? Do you have any last requests?"

"Actually, Sylvia, I do have one. I would sure love one of your delicious, homemade chocolate chip cookies."

"Oh, c'mon Mort," Sylvia answers. "I was saving those for the wake."

Gladys is lying on her deathbed. "Georgie, do you think we can have sex one more time before I die?" she asks. He obliges.

About a half hour later, Gladys says, "Oh, that was wonderful—and I'm feeling pretty good—could we do it once more?" Again, her Georgie obliges.

Around midnight, Gladys whispers, "Georgie, honey, pretty please? Once more?"

George jumps up and says, "Listen, Gladys: ONE OF US has to get up in the morning!"

An archaeologist is the best husband a woman can have; the older she gets, the more interested he is in her. —Agatha Christie

Stewardess: I'm sorry, Mr. Smith, but we left your wife behind in London.
Mr. Smith: Thank goodness!
I thought I was going deaf!

A geezer walks up to a beautiful woman in a shopping mall. "Excuse me" he says, "but I've lost my wife somewhere in the mall. Could you please help me?"

"What do you need me to do?" asks the woman.

"Just stand here and talk to me."

"How's that going to help?"

"I have no idea, really . . . but every time I talk to a beautiful woman like you, my wife appears out of nowhere!"

An eighty-year-old woman marries an eighty-five-year-old man. One day, she isn't feeling very well so she goes to her doctor. Upon examining her, the doctor says, "Congratulations Mrs. Jones, you're going to be a mother."

"Knock it off, doctor, I'm eighty," she says.

"I know! This morning, I would have said it was impossible, but there's no doubt about it! It's a medical miracle!"

"Damn it!" she says, and storms out of the office, leaves the building, and goes directly to a pay telephone. In a rage, she dials her husband.

"Hello" she hears him say, in his familiar, querulous voice.

"You rotten bastard. You got me pregnant!"

There is a pause on the line. "Who's calling, please?"

A young man watches as an elderly couple sits down to lunch at McDonald's. He notices that they order one meal and an extra drink cup. The gentleman carefully divides the hamburger in half then counts out the fries, one for him, one for her, until each has half of them. Then he pours half of the soft drink into the extra cup and sets that in front of his wife. The old man begins to eat and his wife sits watching, her hands folded in her lap.

Finally, the young man feels he has to speak up. "Excuse me, but I hate to see you sharing a meal like that. Can I buy you another Extra Value Meal?"

"Oh, no. No thanks, sonny," says the old man. "We've been married fifty years, and everything has always been and will always be shared, fifty-fifty."

"I understand," says the young man, "but ma'am, why aren't you eating, too?"

"Because, sonny, it's his turn with the teeth!"

Sex at age ninety is like trying to shoot pool with a rope. —George Burns

A noted sex therapist realizes that people often lie about the frequency of their sexual encounters, so he devises a test to determine the truth. He fills an auditorium with people and goes down the line one by one, asking each person to smile. Based on the size of the person's smile, the therapist is able to guess accurately how often they have sex.

Finally, he comes to the last man in line, an elderly gentleman who is grinning from ear to ear.

"Twice a day," the therapist guesses. He is surprised when the man says no.

"Once a day, then? Once a week?" To each question the elderly gent shakes his head.

Finally, the doctor asks the old man to 'fess up, and the man says, "I have sex once a year."

"What the heck are you so happy about, then?" the therapist asks.

"Tonight's the night!"

A couple goes out to dinner to celebrate their fiftieth wedding anniversary. On the way home, she notices a tear in his eye. "Aww, sweetie, are you getting all sentimental because we're celebrating fifty wonderful years together?"

"No," he replies. "I was thinking about the time before we got married. Your father threatened me with a shotgun and said he'd have me thrown in jail for fifty years if I didn't marry you. Tomorrow I would've been a free man!"

An old man wanders into the Social Security office to sign up for benefits. The clerk asks for proof of his age. He reaches for his wallet and realizes, embarrassed, that he has left it at home.

The clerk says, "Don't worry, just open your shirt. If your chest hair is gray, you qualify."

The man gamely opens his shirt and the clerk signs him up for benefits.

Upon arriving home, he tells the story to his wife. "Too bad they didn't ask you to drop your pants," she says. "You'd qualify for disability, too!"

While on a trip to visit the grandkids, an elderly couple stops at a roadside restaurant for lunch. The woman leaves her glasses on the table but she doesn't notice until quite a while later. They have no choice but to go back to the restaurant, and the husband fusses and complains the whole way back, calling his wife every bad name he can think of.

They finally arrive at the restaurant. As the woman gets out of the car to retrieve her glasses, the man yells, "While you're in there, you might as well get my hat, too!"

At a party an older couple is talking to a young one. The young man says to the old man, "I've heard that when you get on in years, you can't have sex anymore."

"I don't know where you heard that, young man, but we have sex almost every night," the older gent replies.

"Really?"

"Sure. Almost Monday, almost Tuesday, almost Wednesday . . ."

There are three great friends: an old wife, an old dog, and ready money.
—Benjamin Franklin

Two oldsters are lying in bed one night. The husband is falling asleep but the wife is in a romantic mood and wants to talk.

"You know, snookums," she says, "you used to hold my hand when we were courting." Wearily he reaches across the sheets and takes her gnarled hand in his own for a few seconds, then tries to get to sleep.

A few moments later she says, ". . . then you used to kiss me." Mildly irritated, he leans in and gives her a peck on the cheek, then settles back down to sleep.

Thirty seconds later she says, ". . . then you used to nibble on my neck."

Angrily, he throws the covers back and climbs out of bed.

"Where are you going?" she asks.

"To get my teeth!"

An old woman goes to visit her daughter and finds her naked, waiting for her husband.

"Why are you naked?" the mother asks.

"This is the dress of love."

When the mother returns home, she strips naked and waits for her husband in the rocking chair. When he arrives, he is startled and asks, "Why on earth are you naked, woman?"

"This is the dress of love," she coos.

"Hmmm," he says. "I think you need to break out the iron."

Ma and Pa are rocking on the front porch when Pa turns and slaps Ma. "What the hell was that for?!" Ma asks.

"That was for forty years of bad sex!"

Moments later, Ma hauls off and cracks Pa right across the cheek.

"Say . . . what?" he asks.

"That was for knowing the difference!"

Married for forty years and counting, Selma and Joe are sitting at the kitchen table. Joe's got the adding machine out and is grumbling, as usual, about finances. "Selma, things are worse than ever," he says. "I don't know what we're going to do! Gas prices have gone up, taxes . . . and Social Security just doesn't cover it. I'm afraid you're going to have to go out and sell your body."

"What?! Are you kidding! I couldn't do that!"

"I'd do it, but I can barely get out of bed in the morning," Joe answers. "You're much more spry than I am. Besides, how many customers would I get as I walked the streets with my walker."

Selma sighs. "Well, okay, if we have no other choice." She gussies herself up with lipstick and hairspray and ventures out.

Some nine hours later, Selma shuffles in. She seems tired but triumphant. "Great news, Joe. I got $47.29!"

"Who gave you the 29 cents?" Joe asks.

"Everybody!" she says.

A couple, both seventy-seven, go to a sex therapist's office. "What can I do for you?" the doctor asks.

"Will you watch us have sexual intercourse?" the man asks. "We think something might be wrong." The doctor agrees. The pair disrobes and quickly go at it, right on the doctor's desk, while he observes.

Upon completion, the doctor says, "There's nothing wrong with the way you have intercourse." He charges them $32.

The two come back the following week, and the following. Each week, they make an appointment, show up at the appointed hour, have sex with no apparent problems, get dressed, pay the doctor, and leave. After almost two months of this routine, the doctor finally asks, "Just exactly what are you trying to find out?"

"Oh, we're not trying to find out anything. We're living with our daughter and we never get any privacy. The Holiday Inn charges $60. The Hilton charges $78. We do it here for $32 and I get $28 back from Medicare."

A couple is sitting at the breakfast table one morning when the old gentleman says to his wife, "Just think, honey, we've been married for fifty years."

"Yeah," she says. "It's hard to believe that fifty years ago we were sitting right here at this breakfast table together."

"I know," the old man smiles, "but fifty years ago, we were probably sitting here naked as jaybirds!"

"Well," Granny laughs, "what do you say? Should we get naked?"

The two strip off their bathrobes and night-clothes and sit back down at the table. "You know, honey," the little old lady says, "My breasts are as hot for you today as they were fifty years ago."

"I'm not surprised," replies Gramps. "One's in your coffee and the other is in your oatmeal!"

A husband and wife are celebrating their fiftieth anniversary. On that very special day, a good fairy comes to them. "Since you have been married so long and you have been such good people, I'm going to grant each of you a wish," she declares.

The wife speaks first. "I wish for an around-the-world trip with my Morrie," she says, and instantly she and her husband have tickets in their hands.

It's Morrie's turn. "I wish my Selma was thirty years younger," he says.

Poof! Morrie turns one hundred.

A couple is being interviewed by the local newspaper on the occasion of their golden wedding anniversary. "In all these fifty years, did you ever consider divorce?" the reporter asks.

"Oh, no, not divorce," they reply as one. "Murder sometimes, but never divorce."

Two old pals are playing golf at their local course. One of them is about to chip onto the green when he sees a long funeral procession on the road adjoining the course. He stops in mid-swing, takes off his golf cap, closes his eyes, and bows his head in prayer.

"Wow," says his friend, "that is the most thoughtful and touching thing I have ever seen. You truly are a kind man."

"It's the least I can do. After all, we were married more than fifty years."

**Men have a much better time
of it than women.
For one thing, they marry later;
for another thing,
they die earlier.
—H. L. Mencken**

An old man ventures to Africa to see a witch doctor. He is desperate to find someone who can remove the curse he has been living with for the last forty years.

The African healer says, "Hmm, maybe I can help you—but you will have to tell me the exact words that were used to put that curse on you in the first place."

Without hesitation, the old man replies, "I now pronounce you man and wife."

Old Mrs. Murphy comes home after her doctor's appointment. "I got a clean bill of health," she tells Old Mr. Murphy. "The doctor says I have the legs of an eighteen-year-old."

"Whoop-dee-doo," her husband says, sarcastically. "What did he say about your seventy-four-year-old ass?"

"Actually, he didn't mention you at all."

A lonely widow, age seventy-three, decides that it is time to get married again. She puts an ad in the local newspaper that reads, "Husband wanted. Must be in my age group (70s), must not beat me, must not run around on me, and must still be good in bed! All applicants please apply in person."

The next day, her doorbell rings. To her disappointment, on her doorstep is a gray-haired gent in a wheelchair. He has no arms or legs. "I'm here in response to your ad," he says.

"You're not serious, are you?" she asks. "I mean, you don't even have any legs."

"I can't very well run around on you, can I?"

"And you don't even have any arms!"

"I can't very well beat you, now can I?"

"Good point. But are you still good in bed?"

The old codger leans forward, looks her in the eye, and says, "I rang the doorbell, didn't I?"

***

An elderly couple goes on vacation to Jerusalem. While in the Mideast, the wife passes away. The undertaker tells the widower, "You can have her shipped home for $5,000, or you can bury her here in the Holy Land for $150." The man thinks about it and decides he will have the missus shipped home.

"Why go to all that trouble," the funeral director asks, "when we can perform a lovely service here for considerably less money?"

"Some two thousand years ago, a man died here," replies the man, "and three days later he rose from the dead. I just can't take that chance."

A mature gentleman is wandering around a supermarket calling out, "Crisco, Cris–co!"

Finally a store clerk approaches him. "Sir, the Crisco is in aisle five."

"Oh," replies the old guy, "I'm not looking for cooking Crisco, I'm calling my wife."

"Your wife's name is Crisco?"

"Nah! I only call her that when we come to the supermarket."

"Oh? Well, what do you call her when you're at home?"

"Lard-ass."

An elderly couple is in a dingy theater, watching a porn movie over and over. After the last showing of the day, the usher who is cleaning the theater can't resist saying to them, "You folks must have really enjoyed the show."

"Not at all," the elderly gent says. "It was disgusting."

"Revolting," adds his wife.

"Then why did you sit through it so many times?"

"We had to! We had to wait until the house lights came up," the missus responds. "We couldn't find my underpants, and my husband's teeth were in them."

Chapter 7
DIVORCE
Good while it lasted...sorta

Whatever you look like, marry a man your own age—
as your beauty fades, so will his eyesight.
—Phyllis Diller

**Getting divorced just because you
don't love a man is almost as silly as
getting married just because you do.
—Zsa Zsa Gabor**

My Dearest Catherine,

Sweetie of my heart, love of my life. My world has
been so desolate ever since our separation. Simply
put, I'm devastated. Won't you please consider
coming back to me? You hold a place in my heart no
other woman can fill. I will never find another
woman quite like you. I need you so much. Won't
you forgive me and let us make a new beginning? I
love you so.

Yours always and truly,
Henry

P.S. Congratulations on winning the lottery.

Divorce: The future tense of marriage.

My wife has tried to change me ever since our wedding day. She got me to exercise daily, improve my diet, stop drinking, quit smoking. She taught me how to dress well, enjoy the fine arts and gourmet cooking, and how to invest in the stock market. I even paint and write poetry.

Now I want a divorce. I'm so improved, she's not good enough for me anymore.

Divorce Redneck Style
"He keeps a goat in the bedroom
and I can't stand the smell any longer."
"Why don't you open a window?"
"What, and let my chickens out?"

Why is divorce so expensive?
Because it's worth it.

A ninety-year-old couple go to court and they say,
"Judge, we want a divorce."
"Folks, you've been married seventy years,"
says the judge, "and now you want to get a divorce?
Why did you wait so long?"
"We were waiting until the kids were dead!"

For sale: wedding dress, size 12.
Worn once—by mistake.

There are two times when a man
doesn't understand a woman:
Before marriage and after marriage.

**Whenever I date a guy, I think:
Is this the man I want my children
to spend their weekends with?
—Rita Rudner**

A traveling salesman is testifying in divorce proceedings against his wife. His attorney says, "Please describe the incident that first caused you to entertain suspicions regarding your wife's infidelity."

The salesman answers, "I'm on the road during the week so naturally, when I am home on weekends, I'm particularly attentive to my wife. One Sunday morning, we were in the middle of a passionate session of lovemaking when the old lady in the apartment next door pounded on the wall and yelled, 'It's bad enough you have to go at it all week. Can't you at least stop the racket on the weekend?!'"

A divorce court judge says to a husband, "Mr. Perry, I have reviewed this case very carefully and I've decided to give your wife eight hundred dollars a week."

"That's very fair, your honor," Perry replies. "And every now and then I'll try to send her a few bucks myself."

Doug marries a woman who is an identical twin. Less than a year later, he is in court filing for a divorce.

"Tell the court why you want a divorce," says the judge.

"Well, your honor, every once in a while my sister-in-law comes over for a visit, and because she and my wife look exactly alike, I end up making love to her by mistake," says Doug.

"Surely there must be some difference between the two women," says the judge.

"There sure is, Your Honor! That's why I want the divorce!"

Mrs. Nussbaum appears before the judge in a divorce action.

"How old are you?" asks the judge.

"Thirty-five," she replies.

Noting her gray hair and wrinkled cheeks, he says, "May I see your birth certificate?"

Without a word, she hands him the document.

"Madam," he says severely, "according to this certificate you are not thirty-five but fifty."

"Your honor," replies Mrs. Nussbaum, "the last fifteen years I spent with my husband, I'm not counting. You call that a life?"

A man appears before a judge to ask for a divorce. The judge quietly reviews the papers and says, "Please tell me why you are seeking a divorce."

"Your Honor," the man says, "I live in a two-story house."

"What kind of a reason is that? What is the big deal about a two-story house?"

"Well, Judge, one story is 'I have a headache' and the other story is 'It's that time of the month.'"

My husband and I divorced
because of our religious differences.
He thought he was God, and I didn't.

Jack is telling his friends about his recent divorce:
"She divorced me for religious reasons.
She worshiped money and I didn't have any."

Did you hear about the man
who divorced his wife because of illness?
He got sick of her.

My husband and I split up.
I finally faced the fact that we're incompatible.
I'm a Virgo and he's an idiot.

**I'm a big opponent of divorce.
Why leave the nut you've got for one
you don't know? —Loretta Lynn**

What do you call a woman without an asshole?
Divorced.

What's the difference between
getting a divorce and getting circumcised?
When you get a divorce,
you get rid of the whole prick.

What's the quickest way to lose
190 pounds of ugly fat?
Divorce him.

Why are hurricanes often named after women?
When they show up they're wet and wild,
and when they go, they take your house and car.

Alimony: The screwing you get
for the screwing you got!

**Paying alimony is like feeding hay
to a dead horse. —Groucho Marx**

Ninety percent of men kiss their wife
good-bye when they leave the house.
Ten percent kiss their house goodbye
when they leave the wife.

If you saw your ex-wife and her lawyer
drowning in a swimming pool,
would you go to lunch or the movies?

The foreman at a Florida lemon grove was interviewing a woman looking for a job.

"Look, lady," said the foreman, "You seem way too qualified for this job. Have you any actual experience in picking lemons?"

"Well, as a matter of fact, yes! I've been divorced three times."

A Woman's Perfect Breakfast

Your son's picture is on the box of Wheaties.
Your daughter is on the cover of *Fortune*.
Your boyfriend is on the cover of *Playgirl*.
Your husband is on the back of the milk carton.

Instead of getting married again,
I'm just going to find a woman I don't like and
give her a house. —Lewis Grizzard

Two recently marrieds are not getting along very well. They are trying to decide whether to get a divorce or indulge in a two-week getaway to Hawaii to try to patch things up. Ultimately, they decide that a vacation will be over in two weeks—but a divorce is something they will always have.

What should you do if you see your ex-husband rolling around in pain on the ground?
Shoot him again.

Divorce is like passing a kidney stone.
It hurts like hell, takes what seems like forever, results in an enormous bill, and at the end you have a useless hunk of rock to show off.

You know it's a bad day
when your blind date is your ex-wife.

Why do divorced men get married again?
Bad memory.

A second marriage is the triumph
of hope over experience.

The happiest time in a man's life is that
period between his first and second marriage.
The problem is . . . he doesn't realize it,
until the second marriage!

Love is the quest, marriage is the conquest,
divorce is the inquest.

How is an ex-husband like an inflamed appendix? While you have it, it causes you a lot of pain. Once it is gone, you find out you didn't need it anyway!

What do you call a woman who has lost 95 percent of her intelligence? Divorced.

Marriage is grand. Divorce is about ten grand.

**Ah yes, divorce.
From the Latin word meaning
"to rip out a man's genitals through
his wallet." —Robin Williams**

What's the fastest way to a cheating man's heart? Through his chest with a sharp knife.

Nuns are women who marry God.
If they divorce Him, do they get half the universe?

Marriage still confers one very special privilege:
Only a married person can get divorced.

My ex was a heart surgeon.
She ripped my heart out.

Marriage: five minutes to get in
and a lifetime to get out.

My wife ran off with my best friend.
Damn, do I miss him.

There was this man who muttered a few words
in the church and found himself married.
A year later he muttered something in his sleep
and found himself divorced.

"I bought my ex a gift for her birthday but she didn't
use it so I'm not going to get her another."
"What did you get her?"
"A cemetery plot!"

We were very happily married for eight months.
Unfortunately, we were married for ten years!

**I was always a marvelous housekeeper.
Every time I left a man I kept his house.
—Zsa Zsa Gabor**

With the divorce rate so high in America, a new organization has been formed called, "Marriage Anonymous." Whenever a man feels like getting married, they send over a woman wearing a torn housecoat, with curlers in her hair and cream on her face, and she tries to nag him out of it.

Sam meets Doug at a bar after his day at divorce court. "So your wife got her divorce ... did the judge split everything fairly between you? asks Sam.

"Sort of," Doug replies. "She got to keep the house, the car, the boat, the furniture, and the dog. I got to keep what I was wearing and what's inside of it."

I've had two unhappy marriages.
My first wife divorced me
and my second wife wouldn't.

Jill goes to her local bank, walks into the manager's office, and says, "I want a loan, I'm going to divorce my husband."

"Oh, we don't give loans for divorces," the manager says. "We offer loans only for things like real estate, appliances, automobiles, businesses, home improvement—"

Jill interrupts: "Stop right there. This definitely falls into the category of 'Home Improvement.'"

A husband, desperate to end an argument, offers to buy his wife a new car. She curtly declines, saying, "That's not quite what I had in mind."

Frantically he offers her a new house. Again she rejects his offer, saying "That's not quite what I had in mind."

Curious, he asks, "Well . . . what did you have in mind?"

"I'd like a divorce."

"I hadn't planned on spending quite that much."

A guy calls up his ex-wife, disguises his voice, and asks to speak to himself.

"Sorry, he doesn't live here anymore. We're divorced!"

Next day, he does the same thing with the same results.

He repeats this every day for a week, until finally his ex-wife figures out that it's him.

"Look, Bozo!" she screams into the phone. "We're divorced! Finito! End of story! When are you going to get that through your fat head?"

"Oh, I know! I just can't hear it enough!"

My mother-in-law broke up my marriage. My wife came home from work one day and found me in bed with her. —Lenny Bruce

What's the only thing divorce proves?
Whose mother was right in the first place.

Have you heard of the new doll called Divorce Barbie?
She comes with all of Ken's stuff.

Divorce, *n*. A bugle blast that separates the combatants and makes them fight at long range. —Ambrose Bierce

Rose goes to see Max, her lawyer, and says, "I want to divorce my Harry."

"Why do you want to do that?" Max asks, "I thought you said he was a man of rare gifts."

"He is," replies Rose. "He's never given me a gift in twenty years of marriage."

"Very funny, Rose. Is there another reason you want a divorce?"

"Yes there is. It's because of his appearance."

"That's an unusual reason."

"Not really. He hasn't put in an appearance at home for four years."

What do a hurricane, a tornado,
a fire, and a divorce have in common?
They are four ways you can lose your house!

Marriage is the sole cause of divorce.

Frank walks into the post office and sees a middle-aged, balding man standing at the counter methodically placing "love" stamps on bright pink envelopes with hearts all over them. The man then takes out a perfume bottle and starts spraying scent all over the letters.

Frank's curiosity gets the better of him. He goes up to the man and asks him what he is doing.

"I'm sending out a thousand Valentine cards signed, 'Guess who?' "

"But why?"

"I'm a divorce lawyer."

**I've never been married,
but I tell people that I'm divorced
so they won't think something's
wrong with me. —Elayne Boosler**

After thirty years of marriage, Howard announces he wants a divorce. Helen is stunned.

"But Howard," she says, "how could you possibly want to divorce me after all we've been through? Remember how just after we met, you caught malaria and nearly died, but I nursed you back to health? And remember when your family was wiped out in that hurricane and I suggested we take them all in until they were back on their feet? Remember when you were falsely accused of armed robbery—and I was the one and only person who stood by you and persuaded the judge to let you go? Remember when you lost fifty thousand dollars to that bookie and I supported you for the next five years? And remember when a fire destroyed your office and I let you turn our den into a home office and worked as your secretary for nothing? How could you leave me? We've been through so much!"

"That's the problem, Helen. Face it, you're just bad luck."

A farmer walks into an attorney's office.

Attorney: May I help you?

Farmer: Yeah, I want me one of them dayvorces.

Attorney: Do you have any grounds?

Farmer: Hell, yeah. I got about 140 acres.

Attorney: No, what I mean is, do you have a case?

Farmer: No, I don't have a Case, but I have a John Deere.

Attorney: I mean, do you have a grudge?

Farmer: Yeah, I got a grudge. That's where I park my John Deere.

Attorney: No sir, I mean do you have a suit?

Farmer: Yes sir, I got a suit. I wear it to church every Sunday.

Attorney: Well, sir, does your wife beat you up or anything?

Farmer: No sir, we both get up about four thirty.

Attorney: Okay, let me put it this way. WHY DO YOU WANT A DIVORCE?

Farmer: Well, the truth of it is, I can never have a meaningful conversation with the woman!

I haven't talked to my wife in three days.
I didn't want to interrupt her.
—Henny Youngman

EPILOGUE
SOMETHING BORROWED, A FEW THINGS "BLUE"

Marriage is made in heaven.
So are lightning and thunder.
—Anonymous

By all means, marry.
If you get a good wife,
you'll become happy;
if you get a bad one,
you'll become a philosopher.
—Socrates

So, here you are. You've survived this book, I hope with your marriage intact. In a few short pages, you've come full circle, from "Oh-honey-bunny-lovey-dovey-kiss-kiss" to "Uggh, are you still here?" to "What happened—she was here a minute ago." And along the way, you visited the many ups and downs on the matrimonial journey. If you are engaged or newly betrothed—

good for you! Don't take any of this too seriously—it's all in fun. (Sure it is.) If you've been married for decades, maybe this helped you find your misplaced sense of humor. It's probably right next to your false teeth and toupee.

The point is . . . okay, there is no point. Except maybe that when it comes to marriage, you might as well laugh. It couldn't hurt—and sometimes it helps! Laughing at your spouse is fun—but laughing at yourself is probably a better bet. Give your poor spouse a break. After all, who else would put up with all of your crap? Life's too short to be miserable—so be glad you've found someone to share it all with, and enjoy every second you've got.

Grow old with me.
The best is yet to be.
—John Lennon

ABOUT THE AUTHOR

Hugh Payne is the author/compiler of several books, including *Yo' Mama Is So ...* He is a grouchy, disagreeable bastard so it might surprise you to know that he is married—though probably not for long, once the missus takes a look at this book. He spends his spare time incinerating ants with a magnifying glass and dragging his fingernails across blackboards. He lives in New Jersey—which might explain his perpetual bad mood.